Uncertain Horizons

The Future Of The Gulf In A Shifting World Order

Bernard Badie, Chedli Mustapha

Global East-West. London

Copyright © 2025 by Bernard Badie and Chedli Mustapha

The Mediterranean Notebooks. A Global East-West Series.

The opinions expressed in this book are those of the author and do not represent in any way Global East-West LTD or The Voice of the Mediterranean.

All rights reserved.

No portion of this book may be reproduced in any form without written permission from the publisher or author, except as permitted by copyright law.

Contents

1. Introduction — 1
   Setting the Stage for a New Era
2. Historical Context — 19
   The Gulf's Role in Global Politics
3. Hydrocarbon Dependency and Economic Diversification — 39
4. Security Dilemmas — 57
   Alliances, Arms, and Autonomy
5. Geopolitical Tensions — 77
   Navigating Relations with Iran and Israel
6. The Impact of Global Energy Transition on the Gulf — 93
7. Environmental Challenges — 113
   Climate Change and Sustainable Futures
8. Socio-Political Dynamics — 133
   National Identity and Popular Sentiment

9. Regional Integration   153
   Opportunities and Obstacles

10. Scenarios for the Future   171
    Risks and Resilience

11. Policy Implications   189
    Strategic Choices for Gulf Leaders

12. Conclusion   209
    Uncertain Horizons and the Path Forward

About the authors   227

1
Introduction
Setting the Stage for a New Era

Defining the Modern Gulf: An Overview

The Gulf's evolving area of interest is the result of changing modern issues. Located at the crossroads of three continents, the Gulf has long been of interest to empires and countries alike. Beyond its geospatial importance, the Gulf is also renowned for its oil and gas reserves. The Gulf region is renowned for supplying hydrocarbons that impact global politics and the economy. Apart from this, the Gulf is also important from a geographical point of view due to its maritime routes. These enhance economic access to trade markets. For these reasons, it is crucial that this region is secured and stabilised. In addition to the above, the region's strategic importance is also increasing due to intensifying competition in the Gulf area. Now more than ever, the Gulf region requires negotiation and consensus on two critical fronts: the influence of overseas powers, and the impact of local powers in securing their needs.

Driven by the aspirations of a young population, rapid urbanisation and technological progress, the Gulf's profile has recently been shaped by social and cultural changes. Gulf regions and societies have undergone consistent evolution, reshaping their societal structures and amplifying their global voice and innovative strategies towards diversification and sustainable development. This requires an analysis of the Gulf's strategic relevance in current global diplomacy through the lens of modern globalisation, combined with historical geoeconomic frameworks that include socioeconomic systems, cultural change and the Gulf's evolving sociocultural factors and comprehensive modernisation initiatives.

Significance of the Gulf in Contemporary Global Affairs

The region's geopolitical position and its vast energy reserves, coupled with its economic impact, establish its critical importance in the contemporary world. The Gulf region is an economic focal point where trade, commerce and transportation flourish, spanning numerous continents and civilisations. Additionally, the region plays a vital role in oil and gas production, further establishing it as a major player in the international energy system.

Alongside its economic importance, the Gulf's geopolitics are of paramount significance. Its proximity to major global maritime trading routes, especially the Strait of Hormuz, makes it a focal point for international security and naval activity. The presence of significant military and naval bases and other facilities in the region underscores its geopolitical importance in ensuring peace and safeguarding global interests. Furthermore, the Gulf's position in world geopolitics has made it a key arena for diplomacy, political relations, deals and conflict resolution activities involving powerful countries.

Furthermore, the Gulf's role in international relations today extends beyond economic and strategic issues. The region's culture, traditions, society and history also grant it influence over other significant factors. Historically at the centre of civilisations, the Gulf fosters cultural dialogue and exchange. At the same time, the rapid progress made by the Gulf states in technology, scientific innovation and sustainable development has placed them at the forefront of global efforts to combat climate change and promote renewable energies and environmental sustainability.

Furthermore, the Gulf region's connectivity with global financial markets and investment networks has expanded its influence even further. The region's powerful sovereign wealth funds, infrastructure projects, and varied portfolio put it at the heart of international finance, capable of guiding capital inflows and outflows, as well as market activity.

As mentioned above, the Gulf's importance in today's global affairs encompasses the economic, geopolitical, cultural and technological spheres, demonstrating the region's multifaceted nature. Recognising this importance is key to understanding the myriad relationships at play in the modern world, as well as the opportunities and constraints it offers.

Historical Foundations and Evolution of Gulf States

The Gulf states are rooted in the Middle Eastern region. Though they can trace their cultural history back to the early days of modern civilisation, their lifeline is interwoven through intricate webs of socio-economic and political interplay.

This mixture brought about the development of these states, which started as tribal societies and transformed into nation-states. Understanding this evolution is crucial to grasping the region's contemporary realities.

The history of the Gulf states begins long before the discovery of oil and the economic boom it triggered. For centuries, the region was an important intersection for trade, connecting different civilisations and cultures. Maritime trade and pearl diving were vital for the prosperity and interconnectedness of Gulf societies long before the modern era.

The colonial legacy also greatly influenced the Gulf States. European colonisers, especially the British Empire, had a significant impact on the region's politics and governance. The treaties and agreements made during this period continue to shape the political landscape of the Gulf to this day.

The socio-political shift in the Gulf States also involved moving away from tribal governance towards modern, centralised politics. The emergence of ruling families, defined national borders and land ownership furthered the formation of nation-states in the Gulf.

Furthermore, the enormous oil reserves discovered in the 20th century propelled the Gulf states onto the international stage, bringing about a drastic transformation of the region. Alongside this increased global significance came rapid industrial growth and economic development, which reshaped the region's social and economic landscape.

The Gulf States are striving to strike a balance between tradition and modernity. As these societies began to modernise at an unprecedented pace, considerable focus was placed on preserving cultural heritage and indigenous identities. This balance between tradition and modernity continues to shape the social relations and public discourse of the Gulf.

In conclusion, understanding the history and development of the Gulf states is essential for appreciating the complexity and evolution of the region. Understanding the Gulf states enables an appreciation of the region's rich and diverse culture, active politics and aspirations for sustainable development.

Key Economic Landscapes Shaping the Region

The economic landscapes of the Gulf region continue to shape its socio-geopolitical dynamics. As some of the world's leading producers, the Gulf states have long been influential players in the oil and natural gas industry. This dominance has impacted their domestic economies, providing both opportunities and challenges. Historically, dependence on hydrocarbon resources has led to accelerated economic growth, transforming sleepy fishing and pearling villages into sprawling megacities with soaring skylines and contemporary infrastructure. Consequently, the Gulf region can now boast international investment, skilled expatriate labour and modern high technology. Apart from oil and natural gas, the Gulf's access to trade, along with its strategic position, has fostered its emergence as a trade and logistics hub intertwining the East and West. This significantly increases their economic importance. The establishment of financial centres and free zones fosters further entrepreneurial initiatives, serving as a main business centre for the rest of the world. However, these landscapes do have some disadvantages. Constantly shifting oil prices, volatile markets and the scarcity of remaining resources highlight ongoing debates about the sustainability of these landscapes.

Gulf economies are concerned about the need to diversify into knowledge-based industries and sustainable development. While striving to achieve green economic growth, the region is making advancements on the one hand, while trying to preserve the natural environment on the other. Additionally, pressing economic concerns include a growing youthful population coupled with high unemployment and a lack of inclusive development, requiring new and innovative approaches and policy changes. It is crucial for stakeholders and decision-makers to grasp the key issues as they plan for a prosperous and resilient future amid the evolving global economic landscape.

Political Dynamics: Leaders and governance

The region incurred an economic setback, unprecedented in the data released more than a decade ago. Although emerging data does show that Gulf states and other associated regions have heterogeneous political structures across international boundaries, the ruling regimes are less flexible. Structural governance differences have a remarkable legacy intertwined with powerful families. These families and monarchs indeed steer the direction of governance, adopting a unique blend ranging from absolute monarchies to parliamentary democracies. These unique systems provide insight into the continuous, subtle changes in the power relations of the extensive political institution within the Gulf. Persistent leadership, accompanied by ruling elites, has a transformative impact on social processes and relations. Regional dynamics, policies, legislation and sociopolitical strategies are profoundly influenced by strategic decision-making and visionary leadership, resulting in sustainable development. However, development oriented towards vision often leads to enduring dilemmas when setting agendas for change. Shifting leadership can pose challenges such as succession, legitimacy and continuity, rendering political discourse irrelevant over time. These paradigms often disrupt order and bring about transitions in domestic and foreign policies, shifting the prevailing political uncertainties and blockages across the region. The morphology of rule and power relations also has significant, enduring aspects that are foundational to the political structure of Gulf states.

The geopolitical relations of the Gulf states trigger diverse interactions with world powers, impacting international collaboration on regional security and economic development issues. This aspect of geopolitics illustrates the challenges present in Gulf politics, as well as the impact of geopolitical players on the local politics of these countries. Additionally, societal expectations and the demand for reforms coupled with the push for participatory governance shape the intrastate aspects of each Gulf country. These changes have sparked debates surrounding democracy, human rights and social equity, forcing governments to strike a balance between stability and reform. Furthermore, the rapid development of technology and media has transformed communication channels between governments and citizens, broadening the scope of public discourse and political engagement. The Gulf is currently charting its course for the 21st century, which will shape the region's trajectory while profoundly affecting the country's domestic policy priorities, international relations and prospects for partnerships with other countries. Therefore, to ensure the long-term sustainability and prosperity of the Gulf states, it is necessary to have foresight and flexible strategies when dealing with such complex challenges.

Social Transformations: Cultural and Demographic Shifts

In recent years, the Gulf region has undergone social transformations and shifts, including profound cultural changes accompanied by demographic shifts. These changes are due to shifts in the economy, such as diversification and modernisation of social and economic activities. The expatriate population in the region has become more cosmopolitan, reflecting a societal trend driven by the growing foreign labour force. There is a transformation underway not only in the demographic balance, but also in the region's culture. At the same time, indigenous people's perception of their identity is changing, especially among the youth, who embrace global cosmetology while wanting to retain their identity. The gradual evolution of women has also played a pivotal role in the new changes.

Over the past three decades, women have undergone powerful changes, propelling them to new heights and providing them with opportunities in education, work and leadership, thereby improving the region's socio-economic status. These changes have redefined narratives, family dynamics, and community interactions.

As urban areas develop rapidly, they become hubs for social and cultural convergence, driving further societal change. This contributes to an increased shift in the Gulf region's consumption patterns and lifestyle choices. Moreover, new social behaviours are adopted to align with newly developed aspirations. Furthermore, technological advancements have made information more accessible, giving rise to social awareness and dialogue concerning rights and inclusivity. These transformative changes bring numerous challenges, such as balancing cultural preservation with modern innovations and potential friction between tradition and contemporary influences. In order to respond effectively to the issues facing the region in the near future, it is crucial that policymakers, business entities and community leaders fully understand the shifts in cultural and demographic data and trends. Supporting sustainable development that is adaptable while simultaneously fostering social cohesion will enable the Gulf region to thrive. Lastly, fostering social unity, embracing change and showing deference to customs and traditions are all fundamental.

Technological Advancements and Innovation Hubs

The Gulf region has recently become a focus for technological innovation and the use of advanced technology to diversify the economy and increase competitiveness in the global market. This region is of particular importance due to the economic and other changes in Gulf countries, which impact international investments. These technological advancements have resulted in innovations across all fields and have shaped new paradigms of innovation in Gulf countries, enabling the key drivers of innovation to access and sustain these innovations throughout the region.

The Gulf region is rapidly embracing digital transformation and adopting leading technologies such as AI, blockchain and renewable energy, thus fostering a culture of innovation. Global changes in technology and innovation have provided Gulf businesses with opportunities to modernise and innovate. This transformation has also stemmed from newly adopted public and private firm policies regarding research, development, and technological investment.

Dubai, Doha and Riyadh have all established modern districts designated for entrepreneurship, attracting not only new and small businesses, but also multinational market leaders. These modern cities, along with growing support for innovation, have encouraged significant investment, which has promoted the establishment of ventures that are a major source of radical change to working practices. Moreover, this has provided local entrepreneurs with remarkable social services, offering convenience and rewards.

The integration of technology and innovation in the Gulf region extends beyond business and industry to encompass healthcare, education, smart cities and transportation. Implementing telemedicine, smart city solutions, and autonomous vehicles demonstrates the region's commitment to using technology to improve society and urban development.

Additionally, the Gulf's increased investment in R&D reinforces its position as a global leader in emerging technologies. Collaborations with leading global universities and the establishment of centres of research excellence have positioned the Gulf at the forefront of discovery and innovation, enhancing economies based on intellectual competencies.

As the world enters the Fourth Industrial Revolution, the Gulf is poised to embrace technological progress, foster innovation, and redefine development milestones. In the next chapter, we will closely examine the strategic influences and partnerships of the key superpowers shaping the Gulf region.

External factors: Superpowers and Strategic Interests

When studying the geopolitics of the Gulf region, it is important to analyse the external factors influencing superpowers, as well as their strategic interests. The Gulf's location at the intersection of Asia, Europe, and Africa makes it a focal point for world powers pursuing economic and security interests. Superpowers such as the United States, China and Russia have manoeuvred strategically to influence the region and maintain their presence there.

Accustomed to being the dominant power in world affairs, the United States sought to control the Gulf's energy market. To this end, it maintained close military and economic relations with certain Gulf states in an attempt to stabilise the region and secure energy resources. Moreover, China's increased engagement in the region is driven by its energy needs and ambitions under the Belt and Road Initiative, resulting in increased investment and development initiatives across the Gulf. Additionally, Russia's resurgence as an active diplomatic and military power in the region has complicated the Gulf's geopolitics by strengthening the region's defence and energy cooperation.

Confrontations and alliances resulting from struggles for superpower dominance have aggravated ongoing conflicts in the Gulf and changed the nature of security relations within the region. These superpowers, with their well-known strategic rivalries, also serve the interests of militaristic blocs and decisive global players who aim to confront their foes, extend their influence to more regions and secure crucial sea routes and chokepoints that are essential for international commerce. Nevertheless, the competition and cooperation between these superpowers within the region and beyond its borders has a significant impact on international politics, with consequences that extend far beyond the Gulf.

While dealing with these external impacts, the Gulf region must strike a balance between forming mutually beneficial partnerships amid these pressures and upholding its independence, territorial integrity and state sovereignty. In my view, understanding the complexities of these relationships, which are shaped by external factors, is crucial for developing effective policy frameworks and diplomatic approaches that will help maintain stability in the region and leverage the benefits of new alliances. Therefore, when projecting the future of the Gulf region amidst ongoing global changes, it is essential to focus on the engagement of superpowers and their competing strategic objectives and interests.

Grasping Internal Prospects and Hurdles

The Gulf states face a number of internal challenges and opportunities that define their socio-economics and politics. Within this framework, the countries of the Gulf Cooperation Council (GCC) must cope with the need to diversify their economies, manage social change and develop social capital amidst political shifts and regional developments. A key challenge for the region is overcoming dependency on oil revenues and developing sustainable, knowledge-driven economies. Additionally, human capital, innovation and non-oil sectors such as technology, healthcare and renewables require investment. The accelerating youth demographic in the Gulf presents both a challenge and an opportunity. Skills enhancement and employment empowerment initiatives are needed to help this demographic become productive catalysts for progress rather than potential unrest. Additionally, gender equity, cultural identity, and social integration gaps remain open problems demanding ongoing attention and funding. In order to address these challenges and fully harness the opportunities, the Gulf states must build cohesive societies that do not discriminate on the basis of gender, nationality, or other ethnic considerations. Additionally, the Gulf region is seeking economic diversification alongside technological advancement, attempting to strengthen institutional frameworks, improve governance, and cultivate environments that are friendly to foreign direct investment (FDI) to foster sustainable growth. While these difficulties are immense, they also present the Gulf states with tremendous opportunities to transform their societies and economies. With appropriate and timely strategic reforms, the region could act as a catalyst and establish itself as a global partner, adding the Gulf to the list of innovation, entrepreneurship, and sustainable development hubs. Through these actions, the region can leverage its geographical position, natural resources, and population to meaningfully influence critical international conversations on issues such as climate change, technological innovations, and social advancements. To achieve these changes, the Gulf will require committed foresight, collaboration with multiple stakeholders, and proactive investment in social welfare, education, research, and strategic planning. Ultimately, addressing the internal complexities and external opportunities comprehensively and simultaneously will define these regions' trajectory towards prosperity and resilience.

Vision for the Future: Pathways to Progress

Strategically positioned on the global stage in the 21st century, the Gulf region is experiencing tectonic shifts that could lead to progress and prosperity. Rather than focusing solely on perpetuating global changes, leaders from the Gulf region must navigate the challenges of sustainable development and balanced growth. This vision hinges on achieving these goals by harnessing their unique strengths while confronting the multitude of challenges ahead.

The diversification initiative seeks to foster innovation and entrepreneurship, as well as reducing dependency on hydrocarbons, to fuel the visionary goal. To achieve economic resilience and competitiveness, these goals must be met alongside the adoption of renewable energy sources, investment in technology and the promotion of knowledge-based industries. Moreover, sustainable economic growth can be achieved by fostering enhanced regulatory frameworks, a skilled workforce and a business-friendly environment.

Alongside economic changes, the Gulf region must focus on social inclusiveness and improvement. Improving healthcare and education, and empowering women and young people, are all hallmarks of an evolving civilisation. Nurturing imagination, critical thinking and a rich cultural environment is bound to benefit society by creating new leaders and innovators.

Additionally, environmental sustainability must be a pillar of the Gulf's envisioned future. Protecting the region's endemic living systems and securing a feasible future requires reducing the impact of climate change, protecting natural resources and adopting green policies. These objectives will require new approaches involving technology and international partnerships to establish the region as a leading proponent of eco-friendly initiatives.

In terms of international relations, advancing peaceful coexistence, dialogue and partnerships within and beyond the region is crucial for stability and collaborative progress. Through proactive diplomacy and conflict mediation to reach a consensus, the Gulf can strengthen its position as a centre of regional balance and international focus. Furthermore, the Gulf's location and historical connections could be leveraged to establish it as a bridge between the East and West for trade, cultural interaction, and understanding.

The culmination of the 'Gulf vision' involves moving beyond traditional paradigms, fostering innovation, and prioritising sustainable practices in the region's development goals. By integrating economic diversification, social progress, environmental stewardship, diplomacy and interstate relations into the Gulf's vision, a transformative schedule can be pursued to make the region more prosperous and harmonious, and to inspire the whole world.

2
Historical Context
The Gulf's Role in Global Politics

The Genesis of the Gulf States: Early History and Formative Years

The ancient civilisations that existed alongside the Gulf states played a significant role in shaping the region's socio-political landscape. Early maritime trade and independent urban centres were crucial to the social structure and economy of the Gulf states. The diverse cultures located around the Gulf were intricately interconnected due to its geographical significance as a crossroads for major trade routes.

The modern Gulf states underwent radical transformations due to competing empires. The Persians, along with the Sumerian and Babylonian dynasties, underwent one of the most intense conversions due to their unparalleled advancements in architecture, multi-dialect governance and the arts of literature and poetry. The accomplishments of these civilisations established a solid infrastructural foundation for the formation of the modern Gulf states.

While the Arabian Peninsula was the birthplace of Islam, it also underwent significant social and cultural changes. Islam gave the inhabitants of the Gulf a sense of identity and brought them together. This paved the way for the development of early Islamic states that were deeply embedded in the ideals of social welfare, governance and justice, which are still evident in modern Gulf countries today.

The era of tribal confederations, alongside the growth of powerful ruling dynasties, saw the initial emergence of Gulf states. Inhabitants began forming complex alliances to expand their political reach, enabling the development of basic governance systems. At the same time, the informal legal principles and customs that evolved during this period helped establish administrative systems for the Gulf states.

During this time, the Gulf states negotiated intricate relationships with opposing powers, established trade routes and practised diplomacy, taking into account local and international frameworks. These relationships were critical in determining the basis of the Gulf's engagement with the rest of the world and setting the stage for the enduring dynamics of influence and interests.

Colonial Legacies and the Quest for Independence

The former colonies of the Gulf region had a direct impact on its political, social and economic frameworks. The incursion of foreign powers in the 16th century marked the beginning of a period of European influence that left scars on the region. For economic and strategic reasons, the British and Portuguese established extensive trading networks, as well as colonial outposts and strongholds along the Gulf's coastline. The residual effects of this colonial era culminated in a violent shift in power between rulers, accelerating commercial activities and sociocultural exchanges and paving the way for the modern nations that comprise the Gulf states.

As they expanded their control, the colonial powers in the region forced local leaders into a paradox: autonomy versus external power control. The need to break free from a foreign political presence emerged as a defining narrative for every Gulf society when reflecting on their contemporary history. The struggle for political autonomy and an independent culture became some of the most defining aspects of contemporary Gulf civilisation.

The mid-20th century was marked by a systematic attempt at decolonisation, and subsequently became the defining period in Gulf history.

Advocacy for the rights of native populations and the establishment of independent states fuelled nationalist movements. During this period, alliances emerged among Gulf states with the shared goal of liberation from foreign control. The tenacity of these movements, and their eventual success in achieving independence, resulted in the modern Gulf states that we recognise today.

While the impact of colonialism is still evident in the region's politics and economy, the pursuit of independence has instilled the Gulf with resilience, unwavering determination and a steadfast will. The region's recent victories, combined with its past struggles, have shaped its distinct national identity and fostered a unique sense of pride and collective identity among the Gulf people. A thorough examination of the region's history reveals that the impact of colonialism and the struggle for independence are crucial for understanding the Gulf's position in international relations.

The Oil Discovery: Catalyst for Regional Transformation

The discovery of oil transformed the Gulf region and the whole world. Formerly dry and sparsely populated areas became bustling economic centres. Unprecedented investment in the region led to economic development and the construction of modern infrastructure. Now in possession of huge quantities of crude oil and natural gas, the countries in the Gulf became dominant players in the international energy market, maintaining control over world politics and trade. This additional revenue streamlined the much-needed modernisation of these countries, transforming them from agrarian economies into industrial entities in record time.

This period marked the beginning of new socio-economic ventures, which dramatically altered the structure of Gulf societies. The catalyst for urban development was infrastructure, which in turn initiated a change in population demographics due to an increase in job opportunities for workers in the region. Along with the increased revenue came the ambition to establish a national identity, which was manifested through the construction of advanced architectural structures that represented the region's aspirations.

Meanwhile, the strategic value of the Gulf region rose swiftly to remarkable levels as world powers struggled to access its energy resources, thereby increasing geopolitical tensions and intertwining local politics with Cold War competition. Gulf states began to alter their foreign policies, gaining access to lawmakers in superpower countries and strengthening their positions in international diplomacy. The establishment of military basing agreements and other strategic alliances marked the Gulf as a newly contested area of geopolitical rivalry where competing interests often collided with the need for energy security and other ideological confrontations.

Alongside this transformation, the discovery of oil reserves accelerated profound societal shifts towards greater energy-based wealth and global exposure. While the region's development was accompanied by increased spending, it also introduced issues such as the need to mitigate dependency on resources, diversify economies and achieve long-term sustainability. The Gulf region continues to be profoundly impacted by the discovery of oil, reinforcing reliance on hydrocarbons and highlighting the dramatic geopolitical shift shaped by the discovery and industrial use of fossil fuels.

Cold War Dynamics and the Emergence of Strategic Alliances

The Cold War is often regarded as one of the most important events in world history. Within this context, we analyse developments in the Gulf area alongside the strategic partnerships that later emerged. While the conflict between the US and the USSR was evolving, the Gulf states were at the heart of an ideological dispute. Additionally, the Gulf region's fledgling oil industry was also squarely in the superpowers' sights and thus attracted intense exploitation and attention. The US and the USSR attempted to control the region's vital energy deposits, which undoubtedly resulted in the region becoming a battlefield for political competition.

The military and political needs of the world powers, along with the oil reserves, undoubtedly made the region one of the most contested areas. During this period, this often led to long-lasting alliances being established between major world countries and many Gulf states. The US strengthened its relations with Gulf states such as Saudi Arabia and Iran by providing military aid and ensuring regional security in exchange for unhindered access to oil and strategic locations. This resulted in a shift in the political balance of Gulf countries, as well as rapid economic growth. However, it also meant growing reliance on the superpowers.

At the same time, the Gulf became a theatre for proxy conflicts, with local actors being used by superpowers to pursue their own objectives. From the Iranian Revolution to the Soviet invasion of Afghanistan, the Gulf states had to contend with spiralling violence and disorder that embroiled regional conflicts with global consequences. These developments highlighted the region's vulnerabilities and illustrated the complex web of alliances and rivalries that characterised the Cold War in the Gulf.

The Cold War also brought change to the internal order

of the Gulf States. The quest for modernity drove rulers to centralise authority and implement radical social and economic policies. Attempts to balance domestic order with external partnerships often led to complex domestic arrangements, with states siding heavily with one superpower or the other to ensure regime continuity. Such arrangements had long-lasting effects on how these states were formed, as well as on their governance and foreign policies.

Overall, the Cold War context, combined with the subsequent strategic alliances formed in the Gulf, irrevocably shaped the region's history. The Gulf states were profoundly influenced by the interplay of international politics, security needs and economic interests, as well as emerging priorities, resulting in certain developments and creating enduring legacies.

Post-Colonial Challenges and Efforts in State Building

The withdrawal of colonial powers from the Gulf region resulted in the emergence of new independent states that were faced with complex issues simultaneously. These included the construction of national structures and definitive formation of identity and governance systems. Although the legacy of colonialism remained, it was essential to devise a clear strategy to navigate the complicated political, social and economic dynamics.

Among the challenges these countries faced after liberation, the need to forge collective, cohesive, inclusive national identities within multi-ethnic, multi-tribal and multi-religious demographics stood out. This was particularly evident in Gulf countries such as Qatar and the United Arab Emirates, where the leadership sought to cultivate a unique, overarching national identity alongside the richly diverse cultures of the population. Bahrain and Kuwait also struggled to strike a balance between unitary citizenship and historical tribal affiliations and hierarchies.

Additionally, state-building efforts had to be accompanied by the creation of effective government institutions that could maintain law and order, provide public services, and generate much-needed economic growth. The Gulf states undertook large-scale modernisation projects aimed at creating effective administrative structures, legal systems and regulatory frameworks. They also invested in education, healthcare and infrastructure in urban areas to bring them in line with other developed countries, in a bid to enhance living standards and national productivity.

Previously situated transnational geopolitics and border tensions due to politically fragile matters constrained myriad state-building efforts. Saudi Arabia and Oman, for example, faced the immediate challenge of defending their borders while ensuring stability within bordering regions, resulting in cumbersome strategic alliances and sophisticated foreign policy calculations.

Marked by the pursuit of geo-strategic dominance by Gulf states, competing global geopolitical powers unleashed unrestrained interventions while vying for prominence in the Gulf region. The notion of fragmented strategies centred around impact without interference drew its triggers from statecraft characterised by a post-Cold War engagement versus sovereignty trade-off. While attempting to exercise independent control, Gulf state leaders were forced to rely on external powers, compelling them to navigate a complex web of political alliances, resulting in economic losses and political complications.

In short, the Gulf region's unprecedented post-colonial interstate conflicts have led to uncontrollable social tensions and fundamentally transformed state-controlled borders, which has had a detrimental effect on the entire region. Concentrated rivalry and self-seeking state power dynamics erupted, culminating in competition between geopolitical heavyweights. The suppression versus autonomy framework demanded resilience and revealed the urgent need for progressive, visionary leadership capable of fostering clear political identities based on coherent historical narratives.

The influence of religion: Politics and the Geopolitical Framework

Religion has always been a pivotal factor in the politics of countries in the Gulf region. The majority practise Islam, which affects not only their private lives, but also the socio-political life of Gulf societies. The intersection of politics and religion has facilitated the establishment of governance systems, the justification of political power and the shaping of policymakers. Islamic doctrines have long been used to defend social and political leadership, laws and regulations, and societal values. Religious leaders have played a key role in shaping the social values and laws of Gulf states as public moral and ethical guardians.

Furthermore, the interface between religion and politics also touches on other aspects of governance. The application of Sharia law impacts legislative, marital and business activities in different parts of the Gulf. Historically, rulers and political elites have used religious imagery and rhetoric to lend themselves political legitimacy and foster patriotism. The concept of religious national identity has, at times, acted as a unifying factor. However, this has also resulted in internal and sectarian divisions within and between the Gulf states.

Furthermore, cross-border religious networks and movements have impacted politics within specific regions. The development of political Islam and its various ideological components has added to the already complex tapestry of the Gulf region. Consequently, alliances and animosities have emerged among the Gulf states, where clashes between competing religious interpretations and geopolitical ambitions have shaped diverging views.

It is important to note that the relationship between religion and politics is governed by an ever-changing framework of fluid parameters. The Gulf region is now experiencing new sociopolitical upheavals and changes with the emergence of new generations and global approaches that redefine the role of religion in politics. Therefore, in order to analyse shifts in power structures, social standings and interstate relationships within the politics of the Gulf region, it is necessary to understand the interplay between religion and politics, given the region's delicate political landscape.

Conflict and Cooperation: Sailing Through Intra-Gulf Relations

Intra-Gulf relations revolve around an intricate blend of distinct historical, geopolitical and socio-cultural constructs. The constituent states of the Gulf region have experienced phases of both conflict and cooperation, which have had a significant impact on the region as a whole. Furthermore, conflicts and territorial disputes have influenced intra-Gulf politics throughout history. These power struggles, alongside external influences, have defined the scope of intra-Gulf relations.

One ongoing difficulty in intra-Gulf relations is border demarcation and managing conflicting territorial claims. Disagreements concerning land, maritime boundaries and shared resources have sometimes caused diplomatic standoffs and strained relations between bordering Gulf states. Resolving such disputes through negotiations or international arbitration has proven difficult, so it is important for the parties involved to find lasting solutions based on respect and understanding.

Additionally, examining relations within the Gulf reveals intricate interstate competition and a hierarchical order for influence and leadership in the region. The emergence of new powers within the Gulf region has often sparked conflict and competition, as states pursue their interests and seek to exert influence over others. This has sometimes resulted in proxy confrontations and political dealings, making regional collaboration and solidarity more difficult to attain.

Despite these challenges, there is a history of cooperative initiatives and some successful joint projects aimed at promoting Gulf cooperation for stability and development. Some Gulf states demonstrate positive engagement through cooperative action in areas such as security, cultural exchange and economic integration. Inter-state and regional organisations and forums provide avenues for dialogue and consensus, strengthening mutual trust as they address common challenges.

The obligations regarding relations in the Middle East demonstrate the need for careful diplomacy and constructive dialogue, as well as a long-term commitment to reducing friction and increasing collaboration. Although historical differences and conflicting interests may pose obstacles, pursuing shared objectives and realising a common future strengthens the foundation of a peaceful and culturally prosperous Gulf community. With better mutual understanding and collaborative efforts, the Gulf states can address intra-regional issues and work towards achieving harmony and progress for all.

Western engagement: From protectorates to partnerships

Interactions between the Gulf region and Western powers have changed fundamentally over time. For centuries, Western powers have sought to influence the politics of the Gulf region and control its hydrocarbons. These interactions date back to when the West began establishing protectorates over Gulf states, actively controlling elements within their territory of interest to advance political and economic goals. This phase influenced the future prospects of interaction, prompting Gulf societies to establish partnership structures. By the middle of the 20th century, Gulf countries had begun to fight for autonomy and self-governance, moving away from protectorate status towards diplomatic ties and partnership contracts with Western countries. Such partnerships were driven by mutual interests in security, trade and energy, and were reinforced by bilateral agreements and military collaboration. Increased modernisation and development in the Gulf region brought Western powers into closer contact, including in the areas of education, technology transfers and investment.

As the Gulf states sought to diversify their economies and develop infrastructure, Western investment and expertise were crucial in integrating them more deeply into the global economy. However, amidst this synergy, challenges and tensions emerged concerning cultural exchange and ideological differences. Nevertheless, these frictions tended to be resolved through dialogue, demonstrating the flexible nature of the relationship on both sides. The Gulf states and the West continue to collaborate on issues such as regional stability, counter-terrorism and trade. Their relationship is no longer that of protectorates and protectors, but of partners, showcasing a combination of historical, geopolitical and economic factors and portraying the Gulf and Western states as adaptable and resilient amidst the shifting landscape of global politics.

Impact of Major Global Conflicts: The Gulf Wars and Other Conflicts

Conflicts on a global scale have significantly impacted the Gulf region, with the Gulf Wars shaping its socio-economic and political landscape. The First Gulf War began when Iraq invaded Kuwait in 1990. This conflict demonstrated the degree of devastation that oil-dependent economies could suffer as a result of geopolitical instability and military aggression. The Gulf states received attention from the rest of the world as a result of these conflicts, which emphasised the importance of global intervention given their vital role as shippers of energy resources. The subsequent counter-offensive by the US and their allies not only restrained Iraq's authority over Kuwait, but also changed the geopolitics of the Gulf region by increasing the influence of foreign military bases and the countries allied with them.

The months following the First Gulf War were marked by a surge in regional and global diplomacy, designed to prevent further conflicts. However, the First Gulf War set the groundwork for the Second Gulf War, also known as the 2003 invasion of Iraq. During this time, there was ample geopolitical conflict due to growing concerns about weapons of mass destruction, intentional regime alteration and increased dominance over Middle Eastern countries. Once Saddam Hussein's government was overthrown, incessant waves of violence and civil war ensued. This cycle of violence led to an even greater crisis with far-reaching consequences for the Gulf and many other countries.

The effects of these wars were devastating, completely changing the global socioeconomic and humanitarian order. The Gulf Wars, along with the regional instability that followed, disrupted global trade, investment and resource extraction, while causing endless population displacement. Much of the war-induced violence in today's world can be traced back to security incidents that took place in the Arabian Peninsula.

Gulf societies have also experienced the direct and indirect impacts of these conflicts, grappling with demographic changes, public discourse and an evolving cultural landscape. Following the two world wars, the Gulf States had to radically rethink their national security policies, strengthen intra-regional alliances, protect their sovereign decisions and engage in difficult diplomacy, balancing external pressures with internal autonomy. Recognising the persistent ramifications of the Gulf Wars, and their reverberations beyond the region, is vital to understanding the shifting geopolitics and relations of the Gulf states with the rest of the world.

Gulf Integration into the World Economy: Commerce, Investment and Power

Gulf integration into the world economy is the result of various factors and processes, including world geopolitics, the region's strategic location, its natural resources, and its revised policies. Trade has long been a vital link connecting the region to the rest of the world for the exchange of goods. Owing to their geostrategic position, the Gulf States have emerged as modern centres of commerce and trade. Recent advances in transport and telecommunications have made the movement of goods, capital and human resources much easier and more efficient across international borders.

The Gulf region has made significant progress in developing economic and investment infrastructure. The Gulf's sovereign wealth funds and investment authorities have become important players in international markets. Furthermore, the development of appropriate regulatory frameworks and financial institutions has boosted confidence, establishing the Gulf as a hub for financial services and investment. Attempts to diversify away from oil dependence have triggered growth in Islamic finance, fintech, and sustainable finance, making the region more resilient and attractive from a financial perspective.

Apart from this, the Gulf actively shapes the global economy through strategic investments, partnerships and participation in major international initiatives. Gulf states have invested in large-scale infrastructure projects to help integrate critical economic corridors and connect diverse regions. Participation in multilateral organisations and global forums also enables Gulf states to influence international decisions and development priorities, including other developmental efforts.

However, the most important aspect is that the Gulf's socio-economic integration raises multifaceted issues regarding sustainability, innovation, and strategic adaptation. The region must align its economic policies with new global business paradigms such as digitalisation, clean energy, and sustainable development. Maintaining a competitive position for the Gulf in the global economy requires a balance of sound policymaking, innovation, and active engagement with stakeholders.

In summary, the Gulf's cross-border trade and investment integration with the rest of the world is a reflection of the region's historical foundations, creative vision and active engagement in the global economy. As the region moves forward into the more complex, yet exciting, dimensions of the economy, its enduring status as a key player in international trade, finance and geopolitics will transform its standing as a keystone in the international economic landscape.

3
Hydrocarbon Dependency and Economic Diversification

Introduction to hydrocarbon dependency

The concept of hydrocarbon dependency in Gulf countries is closely linked to the region's modern history, influencing economic policies, international relations and societal structures. Since the discovery of significant oil and gas reserves, these countries' economies have relied heavily on revenues generated by extracting, producing and exporting these fossil fuels. This dependence has influenced not only the national economic landscape of these countries, but also had profound global repercussions. The historical roots of this dependency date back to the early 20th century when substantial oil reserves were discovered in the region, resulting in rapid industrialisation and unprecedented economic growth. The countries in question benefited from the new wealth generated by these resources, and their economies became increasingly linked to fluctuations in the global energy market. This gave rise to a development model that was heavily focused on hydrocarbon production. The following decades were marked by the establishment of state-owned enterprises and sovereign wealth funds, which further strengthened the link between hydrocarbon revenues and national prosperity. However, this deep dependence has also exposed Gulf economies to vulnerabilities, with periods of instability and economic uncertainty resulting from oil price fluctuations and market dynamics. Furthermore, dependence on hydrocarbons has repercussions that extend beyond the economic sphere to affect the cultural, social and political dimensions of Gulf societies. Therefore, it is essential to understand the nuances of this dependence in order to grasp the complexity of the Gulf's economic and geopolitical realities, particularly at a time of changing global energy dynamics and calls for sustainable development.

The economic impacts of oil and gas dependence

Oil and gas dependence has been a defining feature of the Gulf region's economic landscape for decades. While it has undoubtedly contributed to rapid economic growth and development, it has also introduced a range of complex challenges and vulnerabilities. We will examine the various economic consequences of this dependence, focusing particularly on its impact on national budgets, employment patterns, and overall economic stability.

Firstly, revenues from oil and gas exports form the backbone of Gulf economies, providing substantial financial resources for infrastructure development, social welfare programmes and public sector wages. This influx of petrodollars has played a pivotal role in the swift evolution of these nations into modern, prosperous societies. However, this reliance on a single commodity makes these economies vulnerable to fluctuations in global oil prices, exposing them to external market volatility and economic shocks.

Furthermore, the overreliance on the energy sector has resulted in an imbalanced economic structure with limited diversification into other sectors. While this specialisation has brought prosperity, it has also hindered the emergence of a more balanced and sustainable economy. Furthermore, the capital-intensive nature of the oil and gas industry has led to workforce concentration in this sector at the expense of others, such as manufacturing, technology, and innovation.

Another important aspect of oil and gas dependence is its impact on public finances. As governments heavily subsidise domestic energy consumption, the fiscal health of these countries is closely linked to the stability and profitability of their energy exports. Fluctuations in oil prices can lead to budget deficits, necessitating austerity measures or borrowing and affecting public spending and investment in key areas.

Furthermore, the dominance of the energy sector has created a sense of complacency, reducing incentives for technological innovation and human capital development. With a large proportion of the population employed in the oil and gas industry, there is a risk of skills stagnating and a resistance to change, which poses challenges for future preparedness and adaptability.

In conclusion, while the economic benefits of oil and gas dependence are undeniable, the associated impacts demonstrate the urgent need for diversification and long-term economic planning in the Gulf region. Addressing these challenges will require strategic foresight, innovative policies and a collective commitment to steering these economies towards a sustainable and resilient future.

Key players in the Gulf energy sector

The region is home to some of the most influential players in the global energy sector. These include national and international oil companies, as well as various other stakeholders. National oil companies such as Saudi Aramco, ADNOC and Kuwait Petroleum Corporation dominate the region's hydrocarbon production and reserves, exerting considerable influence over global oil prices and supply. These state-owned entities drive their countries' economies and play a central role in the region's geopolitical dynamics. Meanwhile, international oil companies such as ExxonMobil, Shell, BP, and Chevron have established strategic partnerships and made investments in the region, bringing their technological expertise, operational efficiency, and capital to the development and extraction of energy resources. Service providers, engineering companies, and financial institutions also play an essential role in the energy value chain, contributing to the smooth operation and expansion of the Gulf energy sector. The complex interaction between these key players highlights the intricate network of collaborations, conflicts, and negotiations that define the region's energy landscape. As the energy transition redefines global demand and sustainability imperatives, these key players are well positioned to navigate evolving market trends, environmental regulations, and societal expectations. Understanding their roles and strategies is essential to grasping the broader implications for the Gulf region and the global energy ecosystem. Analysing their activities, investments, and policies provides insight into the future trajectory of the Gulf energy sector and its interconnection with the broader international energy landscape.

The long-term viability of hydrocarbon resources is a growing concern

Concerns about the long-term viability of hydrocarbon resources in the Gulf region are intensifying as the global energy landscape undergoes significant transformation. Growing awareness of climate change and the need to reduce carbon emissions is putting pressure on traditional fossil fuels, so they must adapt to a rapidly changing market. The Gulf's economic prosperity has long been based on its dependence on oil and gas, but the sustainability of this model is now being called into question. The limited nature of hydrocarbon reserves raises crucial questions about their viability as a primary source of revenue and influence. Furthermore, uncertainties relating to fluctuating global demand, technological advances and geopolitical changes pose significant challenges to the future stability of the region's energy sector. While innovative extraction techniques and exploration methods may extend the life of existing reserves, the fundamental question of sustainability remains unanswered. As energy markets shift towards cleaner alternatives and renewable technologies, the Gulf faces a dual imperative of maximising the value of its hydrocarbon wealth while proactively diversifying its economy. Finding a balance between short-term gains and long-term resilience is essential in order to address the eventual decline of hydrocarbon resources and adapt to a new era of energy dynamics. Comprehensive strategies are needed to manage the gradual depletion of these resources and optimise their contribution to broader development goals, ensuring that the Gulf remains a key player in an ever-changing global energy landscape. In order to preserve the Gulf's economic prosperity in the face of declining hydrocarbon viability, it is crucial to embrace innovation, foster strategic collaborations and invest in sustainable practices.

Economic diversification initiatives

Diversifying the economies of Gulf countries has been a priority since the scarcity of hydrocarbon resources was recognised. Various initiatives have been implemented to stimulate economic diversification, with the aim of reducing heavy dependence on oil and gas revenues and promoting sustainable growth in different sectors. One of the most significant initiatives is developing non-oil industries, such as tourism, real estate, manufacturing and technology. Governments have actively encouraged these sectors by providing financial incentives, investing in infrastructure, and adopting regulatory reforms to attract foreign investment and stimulate domestic entrepreneurship.

There has also been an emphasis on developing human capital as a means of diversifying the economy. Education and skills enhancement programmes have been implemented to equip the local workforce with the necessary skills for a knowledge-based economy. Partnerships have been established with renowned international educational institutions and research and development centres have been set up to encourage innovation and technological advancement.

Additionally, promoting small and medium-sized enterprises (SMEs) has become an integral part of these efforts. Governments have sought to foster an entrepreneurial environment by facilitating access to finance, streamlining administrative procedures, and offering mentoring and support programmes. Encouraging SME growth is vital for developing a dynamic and diverse economic landscape.

Significant investments have been made in infrastructure projects throughout the region as part of economic diversification. These projects include developing transportation networks, logistics centres and advanced telecommunications systems, which lay the foundation for a more diversified and integrated economy. Additionally, the establishment of free trade zones and special economic regions has attracted foreign investors and facilitated trade.

To mitigate the impact of market volatility, sovereign wealth funds are being used strategically to invest in various asset classes, both domestically and internationally. This approach aims to generate long-term returns and reduce dependence on oil revenues, thereby contributing to a more resilient and diversified economy.

In conclusion, the Gulf region's economic diversification relies on a comprehensive approach encompassing industrial diversification, human capital development, SME promotion, infrastructure improvement and prudent financial management. These initiatives collectively aim to develop a sustainable and resilient economy that can withstand global economic shocks and prosper independently of hydrocarbons.

The role of government policies in diversification efforts

Government policies play a pivotal role in driving and sustaining these efforts. Policies aimed at reducing heavy dependence on oil resources require strategic planning, regulatory frameworks and targeted incentives to support non-oil sectors. The government's approach is based on a multidimensional strategy encompassing tax reforms, investment promotion, and infrastructure development.

A key objective of government policy is to foster an environment conducive to economic diversification. This involves fostering a competitive business environment through liberalisation measures, simplifying regulatory procedures and improving transparency, in order to attract domestic and foreign investment. The creation of specialised economic zones, industrial clusters and innovation centres also demonstrates the government's commitment to catalysing diversification.

Governments also play a pivotal role in nurturing human capital and fostering a knowledge-based economy. Investments in education, vocational training, research and development are the cornerstone of policies aimed at creating a skilled workforce capable of driving innovation in various sectors. Aligning education programmes with the needs of emerging industries and promoting entrepreneurship are also part of government strategies for economic diversification.

Effective governance and policy coordination are also essential to mitigate the risks inherent in economic restructuring. Governments must formulate strategies that balance short-term imperatives with long-term development goals. This involves phasing out subsidies, diversifying revenue sources, and implementing prudent fiscal policies to ensure sustainable progress while preserving social welfare.

Governments can also establish partnerships with international organisations, multilateral development banks and other countries, benefiting from their expertise, best practices and financial support for diversification initiatives. Through collaborative projects, governments can strengthen their capacity to address technological gaps, build institutional capacity and accelerate the transfer of relevant knowledge.

Ultimately, government policy is central to creating an environment conducive to economic diversification. By adopting comprehensive and coherent policies, governments can harness the potential of non-oil sectors, stimulate innovation, and create a dynamic and resilient economy capable of withstanding global market fluctuations and contributing to sustainable growth.

Challenges to successful diversification

Diversifying economies that have traditionally depended on hydrocarbon resources presents a host of challenges that must be carefully addressed to ensure success. One of the most significant obstacles is the deeply entrenched nature of hydrocarbon dependence in the social and economic fabric of Gulf countries. Decades of reliance on oil and gas revenues have not only shaped the economic structure, but also the national mindset, creating a culture of dependency that resists change. Overcoming this entrenched mindset requires a concerted effort to change attitudes and perceptions, encouraging acceptance of new sectors and industries. Furthermore, the volatility of commodity prices poses a constant challenge to diversification efforts. Fluctuations in oil and gas markets can undermine the stability of alternative economic projects, making long-term planning and investment in non-hydrocarbon sectors unpredictable. This inherent risk deters potential investors and slows economic transformation. Another major challenge is the need to develop human capital and technological capabilities in non-energy sectors. Transitioning from an oil-dominated economy to a diversified, knowledge-based economy requires a skilled workforce capable of driving innovation and productivity across a range of sectors. To address this skills shortage, comprehensive education and vocational training programmes are required to develop a workforce that can compete in the global marketplace. In addition, inadequate infrastructure and institutional frameworks can hinder diversification efforts further. Inefficient logistics networks, bureaucratic obstacles and legal barriers can hinder the growth of non-energy sectors, prompting governments to invest in modern infrastructure and streamline regulatory processes. Political and social factors also play a key role in creating an environment that enables economic diversification. Resistance from interest groups, political inertia and social expectations are significant challenges that policymakers face when steering their economies towards greater diversification. Creating an environment conducive to entrepreneurship, innovation, and foreign investment requires navigating complex power dynamics and societal expectations. Comprehensive strategies encompassing legislative reforms, targeted investments, public awareness campaigns and international partnerships are needed to address these challenges. Success in overcoming these challenges will determine the Gulf region's future economic trajectory and consolidate its status as a diversified and resilient global player.

Case studies: successes and failures

The analysis of some case studies highlights successes and setbacks in the pursuit of economic diversification in the Gulf region. Examining these cases provides valuable insights into the various approaches, strategies and outcomes associated with reducing dependence on hydrocarbons and diversifying economies. The success stories illustrate situations in which proactive measures and innovative policies have yielded tangible results, offering inspiration to other countries facing comparable challenges. These examples of successful economic diversification demonstrate the importance of visionary leadership, strategic planning and sustainable investment in non-energy sectors. Conversely, the setbacks experienced by some initiatives serve as cautionary tales, highlighting the complexities and obstacles associated with diversification efforts. By rigorously examining these setbacks, we can identify critical factors such as the misallocation of resources, inadequate infrastructure and external market forces that hinder progress. Juxtaposing successes and setbacks enables us to construct a nuanced narrative that highlights the multifaceted nature of economic diversification in this region. Furthermore, comparing these case studies with global trends provides an opportunity to contextualise the Gulf's experiences within the broader framework of international economic development. This comparison enables us to identify best practices, potential pitfalls, and areas for collaboration or adaptation of global models. It also improves our understanding of the unique challenges and opportunities that Gulf countries face in moving away from their dependence on hydrocarbons. Ultimately, our aim is to provide readers with a comprehensive view of the intricacies of economic diversification, using concrete examples to shed light on the way forward for the Gulf region.

Comparative analysis with global trends

In today's interconnected world, the patterns of economic diversification and hydrocarbon dependence in the Gulf region cannot be viewed in isolation. They are closely linked to global trends and developments in the energy sector and industrial landscape. Therefore, a comparative analysis of these trends is essential to understand the position of Gulf economies in the broader international context.

Examining global trends in the energy sector reveals that many countries are striving to reduce their dependence on traditional fossil fuels, increasingly investing in renewable energy in the process. This shift is driven by concerns about climate change, as well as falling clean technology costs. The Gulf region, which has significant oil and gas reserves, faces a unique challenge in adapting to this global trend while maintaining its economic stability.

Additionally, the concept of economic diversification has gained importance worldwide as countries seek to create more resilient and dynamic economies. By studying successful diversification efforts elsewhere, such as Singapore's transformation from a trading port to a global financial centre, or South Korea's shift from manufacturing-based to innovation- and technology-focused economies, the Gulf region can learn valuable lessons.

Historically, economies rich in natural resources have encountered obstacles when attempting to diversify their economic base. Issues such as over-reliance on a single sector, a lack of human capital and complex institutional frameworks are not unique to the Gulf region. These challenges are common to many countries around the world. Through comparative analysis, Gulf countries can identify and adapt best practices to their specific context, thereby accelerating their economic diversification agenda.

At the macroeconomic level, the Gulf's dependence on hydrocarbons has repercussions for global energy markets and geopolitical dynamics. Changes in oil and gas production or consumption patterns in the region affect energy prices, supply chains and international relations worldwide. Understanding these interconnections is therefore essential for developing effective strategies for economic resilience and sustainable development.

Therefore, a thorough analysis of the Gulf's situation

in relation to global trends benefits not only local policymakers, but also international actors. This analysis provides a better understanding of the evolving nature of the global economy and offers a means of assessing the interdependence of regional and global processes. Ultimately, it highlights the need for the Gulf to adapt to paradigm shifts and integrate into the ever-changing global economy.

Finding the balance between tradition and innovation

Having examined the complexities of hydrocarbon dependence and economic diversification in detail, it is evident that the Gulf region is at a pivotal juncture. A comparative analysis of global trends has revealed the unique challenges facing Gulf economies, as well as opportunities for sustainable growth and development. In this final section, we reflect on the balance that must be struck between tradition and innovation to achieve economic resilience.

The global economic landscape is constantly evolving, driven by technological advances, changing consumer preferences and a growing focus on environmental sustainability. In this context, the region's traditional reliance on hydrocarbon resources presents both opportunities and challenges. While the wealth generated by oil and gas has played a pivotal role in developing infrastructure and fostering prosperity in Gulf countries, it has also created a dependency that carries risks due to market volatility and the transition to renewable energy in the long term.

As the world moves towards a more diversified energy mix, the need for innovation is becoming ever more urgent. Gulf economies must leverage their financial resources and human capital strategically to foster the emergence of new industries, revitalise existing sectors and adopt sustainable practices. This transition to a more diversified economy requires bold vision, careful planning, and effective implementation. Governments, private companies and educational institutions must collaborate to foster an entrepreneurial spirit and a knowledge-based economy.

However, the pursuit of innovation must not overshadow the rich cultural heritage and societal values that underpin Gulf societies. Striking a balance between tradition and innovation requires a nuanced approach that honours the past while embracing the future. This involves preserving the essence of cultural identity, promoting inclusive development and empowering local communities to meaningfully participate in economic transformation. Furthermore, leveraging traditional knowledge and expertise can provide a distinct competitive advantage in global markets and enrich the narrative of goods and services produced in the region.

In conclusion, the path to economic diversification lies not in abandoning dependence on hydrocarbons, but in striking a balance between preserving the legacy of the past and ushering in sustainable progress. The Gulf region possesses intellectual, financial and natural wealth which, if harnessed with foresight and unity, could enable it to successfully navigate a future marked by resilience and prosperity. By balancing tradition and innovation, Gulf countries can distinguish themselves in the global economy while preserving their unique cultural heritage.

4

Security Dilemmas
Alliances, Arms, and Autonomy

Introduction to Security Dynamics in the Gulf Region

The Gulf region has long been at the heart of global security dynamics, shaped by a complex interplay of historical, geopolitical, and strategic factors. From the influence of colonial powers to the modern era characterised by rivalry between major powers, the region's security landscape has evolved considerably. Its geographical location at the crossroads of major trade routes, coupled with its vast energy resources, has made it a theatre of conflict between competing interests throughout history.

Security concerns in the region are deeply rooted in its historical legacy, particularly territorial conflicts, regional rivalries, and external intervention. The legacy of colonialism and the subsequent struggle for independence have had a lasting influence on the security policies of the Gulf states.

The quest for autonomy, sovereignty and national identity is often intertwined with broader geopolitical strategies and alliances. In this region, the concept of security goes beyond traditional military considerations to encompass economic stability, energy security, and internal cohesion.

Given the region's heavy dependence on oil, security

policies are closely linked to protecting vital energy infrastructure and maintaining stability in the global oil market. Furthermore, the region's diverse demographic composition and socio-political dynamics require a comprehensive security approach that considers factors such as internal stability, social harmony, and cultural preservation.

To understand the region's security dynamics, it is crucial to recognise the multifaceted nature of the threats and challenges it faces. The emergence of non-state actors, transnational terrorism and asymmetric warfare has added layers of complexity to the traditional state-centric security paradigm. Moreover, the proliferation of advanced military technologies, such as ballistic missiles and unmanned aerial systems, has altered the strategic landscape for security actors in the region.

Due to the interconnected nature of regional and global security, Gulf security policies are influenced by global dynamics in international relations. Interactions between major powers, evolving norms of conflict resolution and the role of regional organisations all contribute to shaping the region's security environment. Consequently, the intricate web of alliances, treaties and security architectures reflects the ongoing quest for stability and autonomy in an ever-changing world.

We aim to provide a nuanced understanding of the complex forces shaping the security policies of Gulf states and their interactions with the broader international order by examining the historical evolution and contemporary complexities of the region's security dynamics.

Historical evolution of military alliances

Over the past century, the Gulf region has been shaped by a complex network of military alliances that have left an indelible mark on its security dynamics. The historical evolution of these alliances dates back to the post-First World War period, when European powers sought to protect their strategic interests and secure control over vital sea lanes and natural resources. The decline of colonial empires in the mid-20th century led to the emergence of independent Gulf states, each operating within a precarious balance of power in an unstable region.

During the Cold War, the Gulf became a theatre of ideological and geopolitical competition between the United States and the Soviet Union. Military alliances such as the Baghdad Pact and the Central Treaty Organisation (CENTO) aimed to contain Soviet influence while providing security to Gulf monarchies and emirates. This period was characterised by a substantial increase in military infrastructure and capabilities across the Gulf, which transformed the regional security landscape.

The end of the Cold War led to a reconfiguration of military alliances in the region, with the collapse of the Soviet Union causing a shift in the global balance of power. The United States emerged as the primary security guarantor, forging close ties with the Arab Gulf states through bilateral defence agreements and arms sales. Meanwhile, the Gulf states sought to diversify their security partnerships by establishing relationships with European and Asian countries to reduce their reliance on a single ally.

Numerous multilateral security mechanisms were established in the region in the 20th century, aimed at addressing common threats and promoting collective defence. The Gulf Cooperation Council (GCC) has played a pivotal role in fostering intra-regional military cooperation, as demonstrated by joint exercises and the formation of a unified military command. Additionally, the Gulf has increasingly aligned with international coalitions, particularly in the context of counter-terrorism and maritime security.

The historical evolution of military alliances in this region reflects the interplay of strategic considerations, regional rivalries, and external influences. Understanding this trajectory is essential to grasping the region's contemporary security architecture and the complex challenges it faces at a time of shifting geopolitical fault lines.

The Role of the United States as "Protector" and Partner

The United States has always played a central role in the Gulf region's security evolution, acting as "protector" and partner to various regional states. Since establishing diplomatic relations after World War II, it has strengthened its role as a key security actor by providing military assistance, conducting joint exercises, and offering security guarantees to its Gulf allies. Its military presence in the region, comprising naval bases, airfields and defence facilities, is a testament to its commitment to regional security.

In its role as protector, the United States seeks to maintain stability and deter potential adversaries, particularly in response to perceived threats from non-state actors and hostile regimes. By providing sophisticated weapons, sharing intelligence and running training programmes, the United States has bolstered the defence capabilities of Gulf states, aiming to ensure their sovereignty and territorial integrity. It has also played a pivotal role in facilitating arms sales and technology transfers, thereby contributing to the modernisation of Gulf armies.

At the same time, the United States serves as a strategic partner to Gulf countries, fostering strong diplomatic, economic and cultural ties that underpin multifaceted relationships. Evidence of the collaborative approach adopted by the United States and the Gulf countries can be seen in their bilateral cooperation on counterterrorism, maritime security patrols, and economic development initiatives. Furthermore, the presence of American multinationals investing in the region strengthens the interdependence between the two sides, promoting economic diversification and job creation.

However, the US security umbrella in the Gulf is under scrutiny in the context of rapidly changing global power relations and demands for more equitable burden-sharing among allies. As Gulf countries navigate regional influences and ambitions, they are seeking to expand their security partnerships beyond traditional alliances, thereby reshaping the dynamics of US engagement in the region. Balancing autonomy and strategic alliances further complicates the US's role as protector and partner in the Gulf, presenting challenges and opportunities for all stakeholders.

Emerging Powers: Russia, China, and Strategic Interests

As the Gulf region undergoes significant geopolitical changes, the influence of emerging global powers such as Russia and China continues to grow. Both countries have established strategic interests in the region, driven by economic, security, and political considerations. Russia, with its historical ties to regional actors and renewed interest in projecting its power beyond its immediate sphere, is seeking to strengthen its presence in the region. This is evident through its heightened diplomatic engagement, arms sales, and energy partnerships with regional states. Meanwhile, China's growing demand for energy resources and its ambitious Belt and Road Initiative are prompting it to increase its involvement in the region. The Chinese government has made strategic investments in infrastructure projects, concluded trade agreements, and bolstered its naval presence to safeguard its vital maritime trade routes. These developments have given rise to a complex network of relationships and rivalries between the major regional powers. Furthermore, Russia's and China's arrival in the region has raised concerns among traditional allies, with repercussions for existing security agreements and alliance dynamics. Their involvement in regional conflicts and disputes has also added an extra layer of complexity to the security landscape. As these emerging powers assert their influence, Gulf countries must carefully navigate their relations with multiple stakeholders in order to preserve their own interests. Policymakers and analysts must closely monitor the evolving role of Russia and China in the region, as their actions have profound implications for the area's security architecture and beyond.

Arms Race and Defense Expenditure Trends

The Gulf region has long been characterised by an arms race, with countries investing heavily in defence to strengthen their national security and assert their influence in the broader geopolitical landscape. This has led to increased militarisation, fuelled by historical rivalries, perceived threats from adversarial countries, and ambitions for power projection. Consequently, Gulf countries' defence spending consistently ranks among the highest in the world, reflecting a sustained commitment to strengthening military capabilities and achieving strategic objectives. The acquisition of sophisticated weapons, including combat aircraft, missile defence systems, and warships, has become a feature of defence modernisation efforts in the region. Gulf states are investing heavily in advanced technologies and maintaining qualitative military superiority. Furthermore, the regional arms race has contributed to the proliferation of arms sales, with major world powers seeking to capitalise on the demand for sophisticated defence equipment to influence the strategic calculations of Gulf states. This further complicates the regional security landscape as external interference in the form of arms transfers and military support influences Gulf states' strategic calculations. Despite the considerable financial resources devoted to defence, it is becoming increasingly clear that strategic restraint and a more balanced approach to security challenges are needed. Therefore, the current debate on defence spending trends must carefully consider its implications for sustainable development, economic diversification, and societal well-being. Going forward, it will be imperative for Gulf leaders to strike a delicate balance between ensuring military preparedness and promoting regional stability while mitigating the potential destabilising impact of an uncontrolled arms race. A nuanced understanding of defence spending trends is ultimately essential for formulating policies that are consistent with the long-term interests of Gulf states and contribute to the broader goal of promoting peace and security in the region.

Arms Race and Defense Expenditure Trends

In the Gulf region, the concept of autonomy as opposed to dependence is a key factor in defining national interests and security strategies. The quest for autonomy often involves reducing dependence on external powers to guarantee security and economic stability while preserving sovereignty and strategic independence in decision-making. However, this quest for autonomy must be carefully balanced, recognising existing dependencies, particularly with regard to global energy markets and geopolitical alliances. Gulf countries operate within a complex web of interdependencies, striving to assert their autonomy while acknowledging the realities of their economic and security ties with external actors. This delicate balance requires constant assessment and adaptation as regional dynamics evolve. A sustainable balance between autonomy and dependence can only be achieved through a multidimensional approach encompassing diplomatic engagement, economic diversification, military capacity building, and strategic partnerships. While sovereignty in defence, trade and foreign policy is fundamental to preserving national autonomy, it must be based on a realistic assessment of international interdependence and the potential repercussions of policy choices on regional stability. The evolving nature of global power dynamics and emerging threats further complicates the challenge of striking this balance. As the Gulf region faces shifting alliances and new security challenges, governments must adjust their strategies to protect their national interests without jeopardising vital partnerships or exacerbating vulnerabilities. Furthermore, developing local capabilities and strengthening resilience are crucial for mitigating the risks associated with excessive dependence on external assistance. This requires an understanding of geopolitical realities, proactive policy formulation and sustained investment in national capacity-building efforts. Effective governance and strategic vision are essential to charting a course that optimises national autonomy while managing dependencies prudently. Therefore, a comprehensive framework balancing national interests should encompass harmonising national development programmes with regional and global imperatives. This would foster a dynamic equilibrium, allowing Gulf states to navigate the complexities of interdependence while preserving their long-term autonomy.

Internal security challenges: stability or reform?

Internal security challenges in the Gulf region are characterised by a complex landscape requiring a delicate balance between maintaining stability and implementing necessary reforms. While prioritising stability and security, Gulf states are increasingly facing internal pressures demanding comprehensive reforms in various socio-political areas.

The traditional approach of relying on the security apparatus to maintain stability is coming up against the need for progressive reforms that address the root causes of discontent and social unrest. One of the main challenges is the discrepancy between the aspirations of a young, educated population and the established governance structures.

Access to information and ideas on a global scale has given young people different aspirations, manifested in demands for greater representation, transparency, and opportunities to meaningfully participate in shaping the future of their countries. However, these aspirations often conflict with long-standing socio-political systems, creating tensions and dilemmas for governments.

Economic disparities and youth unemployment also contribute to social discontent and potential instability. Addressing these issues requires short-term strategies and long-term policies aimed at diversifying the economy, creating jobs, and promoting inclusive growth. Gulf leaders must strike a delicate balance between immediate stability measures and sustainable reforms.

Furthermore, the influence of external actors and regional dynamics complicates the security landscape further. Gulf states are caught up in geopolitical rivalries and regional conflicts that can exacerbate internal security challenges.

To navigate these complexities while pursuing internal reforms, a nuanced political approach and long-term strategic vision are required. Any reform initiatives aimed at strengthening civil liberties, promoting social cohesion and fostering an environment conducive to innovation must be carefully calibrated to avoid potential destabilisation.

At the same time, it is essential to maintain security and protect the country from external threats, which requires robust and adaptable security frameworks. Striking the right balance between stability and reform is crucial for ensuring the long-term resilience and prosperity of these states.

In conclusion, the internal security challenges facing Gulf states require a holistic approach that considers both stability and meaningful reform. Meeting this challenge will require careful planning and the ability to adapt to the region's evolving socio-political landscape, ensuring lasting peace and progress.

Cybersecurity and technological advances

As the Gulf region continues to face complex security dilemmas, one critical area requiring increased attention is cybersecurity and technological advances. In an era of rapid digital transformation and increasing interconnectivity, traditional security paradigms have evolved to encompass the cyber domain. Cybersecurity has become essential for protecting national interests, critical infrastructure and sensitive data from a wide range of threats. Gulf states are increasingly recognising the need to strengthen their cyber defences in the face of escalating cyberattacks and espionage activities.

However, adopting technological advances while managing associated vulnerabilities remains a challenge for Gulf countries. Digitalisation, artificial intelligence, and the Internet of Things (IoT) offer unprecedented opportunities for innovation, economic growth, and societal improvement. However, these advances also create opportunities for malicious actors to exploit systemic weaknesses, commit cybercrime and wage sophisticated cyber warfare. The convergence of the physical and cyber domains underscores the importance of integrating cybersecurity strategies into wider national security frameworks.

Furthermore, cyber threats emerging from both state and non-state actors emphasise the transnational nature of cybersecurity challenges. Gulf states must therefore collaborate with their international partners, sharing information and adopting proactive measures to address these threats. Cooperation through bilateral and multilateral agreements, intelligence sharing and joint exercises can strengthen collective preparedness and response capabilities against cyber-attacks.

At the same time, it is essential to invest in cybersecurity talent, strengthen national cyber defence capabilities, and advance research and development initiatives to enhance sovereign resilience in this area. Furthermore, developing public–private partnerships and leveraging private sector expertise will increase the flexibility and sophistication of cyber defence mechanisms. By cultivating a robust cybersecurity ecosystem, Gulf states can position themselves favourably to address emerging cyber risks and strengthen their presence in the global digital landscape.

Ultimately, cybersecurity and technological advancement require a nuanced, forward-looking approach that balances the benefits of digital innovation with proactive risk mitigation strategies. Aligning these efforts is crucial for preserving the security, stability, and resilience of the Gulf region at a time when the cyber domain is increasingly interfering with traditional security dynamics.

Multilateral Cooperation: Collective Security Frameworks

Multilateral cooperation and collective security frameworks are indispensable for maintaining peace, stability and protecting common interests in this dynamic and complex geopolitical landscape.

In the dynamic and complex geopolitical landscape of the Gulf region, multilateral cooperation through collective security frameworks has become indispensable for maintaining peace and stability, and for protecting common interests. These frameworks are vital for addressing shared security challenges, fostering trust, and encouraging collaboration between regional and international stakeholders. The evolution of these frameworks has been influenced by factors such as historical alliances, geopolitical changes, technological advances, and the evolving nature of contemporary security threats. Here, we examine the importance of multilateral cooperation in developing these frameworks and explore the complexities and opportunities inherent in such agreements.

The development and strengthening of these frameworks requires an in-depth understanding of the region's various security concerns. Traditional military threats coexist with non-traditional challenges such as terrorism, cyber warfare and asymmetric conflicts, meaning security considerations are numerous and varied. Consequently, the architecture of multilateral cooperation must encompass a variety of strategies and initiatives, including intelligence sharing, joint military exercises, diplomatic dialogues, and capacity-building programmes. Collaborative efforts in areas such as maritime security, border control, and counter-terrorism operations are crucial for fostering a collective response to the security challenges facing Gulf states.

Furthermore, the involvement of external actors and international organisations adds an additional dimension to the dynamics of multilateral cooperation in the region. The participation of major powers such as the United States, Russia and China in collective security frameworks has significant implications for regional security. Striking a balance between the interests of regional and international actors requires skilful diplomatic negotiations and strategic alignments. Additionally, aligning collective security frameworks with existing regional bodies such as the Gulf Cooperation Council (GCC) and other transnational organisations enables the development of comprehensive security governance and mutual assistance.

Effective multilateral cooperation also requires pragmatic reflection on the legal and institutional frameworks governing collective security efforts. Conflict prevention and resolution mechanisms, supported by robust legal frameworks, are essential to ensure the legitimacy and effectiveness of collaborative security initiatives, as is post-conflict reconstruction. Additionally, establishing confidence-building measures, dispute resolution mechanisms, and commitment verification contributes to the credibility and sustainability of collective security agreements.

Ultimately, the future of collective security frameworks in the Gulf depends on participating states' ability to prioritise common security imperatives over individual national interests. Although challenges such as historical rivalries, competition for resources, and political differences may complicate the process, the potential benefits of enhanced collective security far outweigh the obstacles. Fostering an environment of mutual trust, inclusive dialogue and coordinated action can lay the foundation for sustainable, resilient security architectures that reflect the Gulf region's evolving realities.

Prospects for Future Security Architectures

The future of security architectures in the Gulf region is both promising and fraught with challenges in this rapidly changing geopolitical context. Several key factors will influence the effectiveness of future security frameworks in maintaining stability and peace in the region.

Firstly, the emergence of new global power centres and the reconfiguration of existing alliances will significantly influence regional security architecture. Evolving international relations, particularly with the rise of non-traditional actors such as China and Russia, will necessitate a re-evaluation of traditional security arrangements and the development of new cooperation mechanisms.

Additionally, technological advances, particularly in cybersecurity, present opportunities and vulnerabilities for future security architectures. The growing interconnection of critical infrastructure and increased reliance on digital systems reinforce the need for robust cybersecurity measures in any future security framework. This includes the protection of physical assets and the prevention of cyber threats that could disrupt regional stability.

Furthermore, the ongoing debate on autonomy and sovereignty will continue to influence the outlook for future security architectures in the region. As regional powers seek to assert their independence and autonomy, the design of security frameworks must strike a balance between promoting collective security and respecting each state's individual aspirations. Achieving this balance is essential to fostering trust and cooperation among regional actors while recognising their specific security concerns.

To address non-traditional security threats such as climate change, resource scarcity and social instability, future security architectures must adopt a comprehensive approach. Understanding that security encompasses more than just military defence, future frameworks must incorporate strategies for sustainable development, environmental protection, and social resilience to effectively address the root causes of instability.

Finally, the future of security architectures depends on states in the region engaging in constructive dialogue and diplomacy. Building mutual trust and transparent communication and resolving historical disputes will be essential to developing resilient and adaptable security frameworks that can withstand the test of time and changing circumstances.

In conclusion, the establishment of effective future security architectures depends on regional actors' ability to demonstrate innovation, inclusivity and cooperation. As it navigates the complexities of new power dynamics, technological advances, sovereign aspirations, non-traditional threats, and diplomatic engagement, the Gulf region is well positioned to develop responsive and agile security architectures that promote lasting peace and prosperity.

5

Geopolitical Tensions
Navigating Relations with Iran and Israel

Introduction to Regional Geopolitics

The region's geopolitical landscape is a complex mosaic shaped by centuries of historical legacy, strategic alliances and contemporary power dynamics. Recent developments in the Middle East have added further complexity to this already challenging region. The rise and fall of empires, territorial conflicts, and the quest for regional dominance have all left indelible marks on the region's political landscape. As alliances shift and powerful new players emerge, a deep understanding of the nuances of regional geopolitics is necessary to grasp the complex dynamics at play. Recent events, such as revolutions, conflicts and peace agreements, have further emphasised the constant evolution of regional politics and its repercussions on the global stage. Additionally, the ongoing nuclear arms race and intensifying arms race continue to fuel tensions and influence geopolitical strategies throughout the region. As external powers recalibrate their interests in the Middle East, the complex web of international relations becomes intertwined with the region's internal complexities, including politics, sectarianism, and socio-economic disparities. To navigate this multifaceted landscape, a comprehensive analysis of recent developments and historical trends is essential. We will examine the interaction between historical tensions and contemporary alliances, shedding light on the intricate dynamics that shape the regional geopolitical landscape.

Historical tensions and alliances

The historical context of the Gulf region is characterised by a complex web of tensions, alliances and power struggles that have had a profound impact on its geopolitical landscape. Over the centuries, various empires, including the Persians, Ottomans and British, have competed for influence and control over this strategic crossroads. The emergence of modern nation states in the 20th century brought new fault lines and rivalries to the fore, often exacerbated by external intervention and the dynamics of superpower rivalry during the Cold War. Historical tensions between neighbouring states, such as Iran and Iraq, as well as intra-Gulf rivalries, have laid the foundations for enduring geopolitical friction. This region's complex web of historical rivalries and alliances has also been influenced by global power shifts and fluctuations in international relations. Significant events such as the 1979 Iranian Revolution and the Arab-Israeli conflicts have further reinforced regional divisions and forged lasting enmities. Furthermore, the legacy of colonialism and the creation of artificial borders has had a profound impact on the region's political geography, contributing to ongoing conflicts and power struggles. Throughout history, alliances in the

Gulf have been unstable and contingent, often driven by pragmatic considerations related to security, economic interests, and ideological affinities. Shifts in alliances and allegiances reflect changing power dynamics and strategic imperatives. Historical alliances in the Gulf region, whether military pacts, economic partnerships or diplomatic agreements, have profoundly influenced its stability and security. To address the contemporary geopolitical challenges facing the Gulf region, it is essential to understand the deep historical roots of tensions and alliances. By delving into this rich history, we can gain valuable insights into the enduring complexities that continue to define the region's geopolitics.

Strategic interests and drivers of conflict

The Gulf region has always been at the centre of strategic interests and drivers of conflict, shaped by complex geopolitical dynamics, historical tensions, and multifaceted alliances. The region's key players have expressed their strategic interests through economic, political and military commitments. Their quest for influence, security and regional dominance has led them to evolve within a complex network of alliances and tensions. At the heart of these interests lie control over vital resources, protection of national security, and preservation of regional stability. Consequently, the struggle for power and influence in this area is inextricably linked to the broader global geopolitical landscape, with implications that extend far beyond regional borders. In this context, the interactions between the Gulf states, Iran and Israel are pivotal in determining regional dynamics. These interactions are fuelled by various conflicting factors, including territorial disputes, ideological differences, and the quest for supremacy. Furthermore, the proliferation of advanced military technologies, particularly ballistic missiles and drones, has significantly increased the risk of conflict and destabilisation. The interplay of strategic interests and conflict factors highlights the need for a comprehensive and nuanced approach, including the search for effective diplomatic and political solutions. It is crucial to recognise the multifaceted nature of these factors, which include historical grievances, ideological rivalries, and contemporary power struggles. Moreover, the involvement of both state and non-state actors complicates the situation further, with non-traditional forces exerting an unprecedented level of influence. Understanding the strategic interests and conflict factors in the Gulf requires studying not only overt actions, but also covert manoeuvres, asymmetric tactics, and the underlying psychology of decision-making. This complex mosaic of factors influences the behaviour and choices of regional actors, highlighting the inherent complexity of managing relations with Iran and Israel.

Diplomatic engagements with Iran

Diplomatic relations with Iran have long been a pivotal element of regional geopolitics, characterised by a intricate interplay of historical animosities, strategic interests and global power dynamics. Gulf states have long sought to maintain a delicate balance in their interactions with Iran, ensuring their own security and stability while managing the multiple dimensions of their relations with Tehran. Iran's growing influence in the Gulf region, particularly in Bahrain, Iraq, and Yemen, has challenged the traditional balance of power and exacerbated tensions, requiring skilful diplomacy.

Against this backdrop, the Gulf states have initiated various diplomatic initiatives to promote dialogue, ease tensions, and mitigate the adverse impact of Iran's regional policies. Bilateral and multilateral dialogues have been initiated to address concerns related to Iran's nuclear programme, ballistic missile development, and its support for non-state actors throughout the Middle East. These engagements have played a pivotal role in shaping a broader regional security architecture, encompassing confidence-building measures, transparency initiatives and the exploration of potential areas of cooperation.

Economic relations have also been an important part of diplomatic engagement with Iran. Despite the imposition of international sanctions, trade relations and economic partnerships between the Gulf states and Iran have continued to develop within the limits imposed by the sanctions regime. Navigating the complex web of economic interactions has required skilful negotiation, risk assessment and the strategic diversification of economic ties, balancing economic imperatives with geopolitical considerations.

In addition to their bilateral commitments, Gulf states have participated in broader international forums that address the challenges posed by Iran's regional behaviour. Participation in multilateral platforms such as the United Nations, the Arab League and the Gulf Cooperation Council (GCC) allows them to coordinate their diplomatic position, express shared concerns and advocate peaceful conflict resolution.

Despite ongoing geopolitical tensions, diplomatic engagement with Iran has emphasised the importance of dialogue and close relations, recognising that stable and constructive relations with Tehran are vital for achieving a more secure and prosperous Gulf region. As Gulf states navigate a rapidly changing geopolitical landscape, managing their intricate relations with Iran will necessitate nuanced diplomatic strategies, adept negotiations, and an unwavering dedication to preserving regional stability and prosperity.

Economic interactions and sanctions policies

At the heart of the complex web of geopolitical tensions in the Gulf region, economic interactions and sanctions policies play a pivotal role in the relations between nations. The intricate relationship between trade, investment, and resource management is significantly impacted by international sanctions regimes and the responses of regional powers.

The imposition of sanctions can significantly hinder economic relations between countries, disrupting established trade networks and reducing foreign investment. In the Gulf context, the repercussions of sanctions are closely linked to the hydrocarbon industry, given its strategic importance in the global energy landscape. Consequently, the evolution of sanctions policy has profound implications for the economic stability and growth prospects of Gulf states, incentivising them to adopt adaptive strategies to mitigate potential disruptions.

Furthermore, the application of sanctions often leads to the reconfiguration of economic alliances and partnerships as countries seek to diversify their sources of investment and trade. This restructuring of economic exchanges can lead to the emergence of new trade routes, financial dependencies, and diplomatic alignments, thereby disrupting the region's traditional balance of power.

Understanding these complex links between the economy and sanctions policy is essential for grasping the global geopolitical landscape of the Gulf. It is also imperative to analyse the strategies implemented by Gulf states to address the challenges posed by sanctions. These strategies include diversifying economic portfolios, strengthening domestic industries, and collaborating with countries that do not impose sanctions.

Exploiting technological innovations and investing in knowledge-based economies are also integral to efforts to mitigate the negative effects of economic sanctions.

Sanctions policies also extend to the financial and banking sectors, where restrictions on transactions and access to global financial systems can hinder the free movement of capital and slow the development of dynamic financial markets. Therefore, Gulf states must establish robust financial systems and regulatory frameworks to withstand the disruptive effects of sanctions and maintain economic stability.

In conclusion, the interaction between economic activities and sanctions policies in the Gulf region is a critical issue requiring careful analysis and strategic vision. The following chapters will explore the dynamic responses of Gulf states to these complex economic and geopolitical challenges in more detail.

Military posture and defence strategies

In the context of regional geopolitical tensions, military posture and defence strategies play a crucial role in security dynamics. The presence of numerous military bases, significant arms purchases and ongoing regional conflicts highlight the strategic importance of military capabilities in this unstable environment. Despite diplomatic efforts and attempts at conflict resolution, the persistent sense of threat has prompted nations to prioritise robust defence strategies to protect their national interests and territorial integrity. The multifaceted nature of military posture encompasses the deployment of forces and weapons, complex alliances, intelligence operations, and technological advances.

It is important to analyse the various aspects of military positioning and defence strategies adopted by the region's key players, as well as the regional arms race, the concepts of deterrence, and the evolving nature of military doctrines in a context of escalating geopolitical rivalries. Additionally, a review of counterinsurgency operations, maritime security initiatives, and cyberwarfare preparedness will provide insight into the region's overall defence frameworks.

Moreover, how external powers influence military dynamics, and the implications of arms sales and military aid for the regional balance is no less important for the analyst. By closely examining the military postures and defence strategies of each Gulf state, the analysis aims to highlight their implications for regional stability and coordination. Through an in-depth exploration of these key elements, a better understanding of the complex network of military dynamics and its ramifications for regional geopolitics will be possible, providing valuable insights for policymakers, academics, and global actors interested in security in the Gulf region.

Navigating the Israeli-Palestinian conflict

The Israeli-Palestinian conflict is one of the most enduring and complex challenges in the region's history. Dating back to the mid-20th century, it has deep roots in historical, religious, and territorial contexts that have shaped the dynamics of the Middle East. A comprehensive understanding of the conflict requires consideration of multiple layers of historical grievances, territorial disputes, competing national narratives and divergent aspirations for statehood and self-determination.

The conflict primarily centres on competing territorial claims between Israel and the State of Palestine. The quest for sovereignty and control over Jerusalem, which is of profound importance to both Israelis and Palestinians, further intensifies the conflict. Security concerns, settlements, refugees, borders, and the status of disputed areas are deeply entrenched in this long-standing conflict, constituting major obstacles to a lasting resolution.

Numerous diplomatic initiatives, peace negotiations and international interventions have been undertaken in an attempt to resolve it. The Oslo Accords of the 1990s aimed to establish a framework for peaceful coexistence and bring peace, but encountered obstacles and limitations. The UN, the EU and other international actors have played a pivotal role in advocating for a two-state solution, emphasising the importance of mutual recognition, security assurances and equitable land division.

Furthermore, the socio-economic dimensions of the Israeli–Palestinian conflict have exacerbated social disparities and created humanitarian problems. These include the impact on livelihoods, access to resources, and the implementation of security measures. These issues are closely linked to the quest for economic development, infrastructure, and pathways to sustainable prosperity within a context of constructive coexistence.

As regional dynamics continue to evolve, the Israeli–Palestinian conflict remains an influential factor in broader geopolitical behaviour and alliances. Understanding the complex interaction between internal, regional and global influences is essential to developing effective conflict resolution strategies and achieving lasting peace. Ultimately, managing the Israeli–Palestinian conflict requires a nuanced approach that considers the complexity of historical legacies and opposing narratives, as well as the search for sustainable balance.

Regional cooperation frameworks

In the context of Gulf relations with Iran and Israel, these frameworks play a pivotal role in shaping the geopolitical landscape. As the region faces complex challenges and diverse interests, establishing constructive frameworks for collaboration is essential to fostering stability and promoting mutual prosperity. Regional cooperation encompasses not only diplomatic commitments, but also economic integration, collaborative security and cultural exchanges. In the current context, evolving geopolitical realities emphasise the importance of cultivating robust alliances and reinforcing cooperation mechanisms within the Gulf and neighbouring countries. Regional cooperation is vital in promoting dialogue, addressing shared concerns, and establishing the groundwork for lasting peace and development. A strategic vision based on mutual respect and understanding can foster an environment conducive to trust and collective action among nations. Key areas for regional cooperation include trade liberalisation, infrastructure development, energy interconnections, and joint environmental preservation efforts. Such collaborative initiatives strengthen economic ties, build trust and reduce tensions, thereby promoting inclusive growth. Furthermore, regional cooperation frameworks provide a platform for resolving disputes peacefully, fostering people-to-people ties and encouraging a sense of shared purpose. Strategic dialogues aimed at promoting regional cooperation must consider the interests and aspirations of all stakeholders while recognising the historical and socio-political specifics of each nation. Through open and inclusive dialogue, regional actors can pave the way for lasting stability and resilience. Adopting multilateral partnerships and cooperation initiatives allows the combined strengths and expertise of participating states to be leveraged to address transnational challenges, such as cybersecurity threats, maritime security issues, and humanitarian crises. To ensure the success of regional cooperation frameworks, participating states must adhere to the principles of good governance, transparency and mutual accountability. By strengthening their ties and deepening their collaboration, Saudi Arabia, Iran and Israel can collectively steer the region towards a future characterised by peace, prosperity and harmonious coexistence.

Final thoughts on diplomatic balance

The complex web of geopolitical tensions in the Gulf region requires delicate diplomacy to manage relations with Iran and Israel effectively. As we turn the page on this chapter, it is crucial to emphasise the importance of maintaining balance in diplomatic relations to mitigate potential conflicts and foster regional stability.

This requires careful adjustments to national interests, strategic objectives, and historical animosities. It requires skilful negotiations, active mediation, and the wise management of alliances and rivalries. The combination of historical tensions, religious influences, and complex power struggles necessitates a nuanced diplomatic approach that considers the sensitivities and aspirations of each stakeholder.

In the Iranian context, diplomatic initiatives must be based on a comprehensive understanding of the country's regional ambitions, its nuclear programme, and its involvement in proxy conflicts. While a firm stance is sometimes necessary to preserve national security interests, channels of dialogue must remain open to explore possibilities for de-escalation and cooperation, avoiding hostility or long-term isolation.

At the same time, the evolution of relations with Israel requires striking a delicate balance between acknowledging legitimate grievances and promoting prospects for peaceful coexistence. Normalising relations with Israel is disrupting the regional geopolitical landscape and requires agile diplomacy to allay fears while exploiting economic, technological and security opportunities.

To strike this balance, regional cooperation frameworks, multilateral dialogues and international mediation mechanisms must be leveraged to promote de-escalation and confidence-building measures. Collective security initiatives, trade partnerships and cultural exchanges can foster mutual understanding and defuse animosity between states, which is essential for lasting peace and prosperity.

In conclusion, the path to lasting peace and stability in the Gulf is clearly linked to balancing diverse interests and aspirations through pragmatic, principled and proactive diplomacy. Pursuing diplomatic balance is a strategic imperative and a moral obligation to preserve the future of the region and its people. This allows us to transcend deep-rooted enmities and forge a shared destiny based on mutual respect, cooperation, and lasting peace.

6

The Impact of Global Energy Transition on the Gulf

Introduction to the Global Energy Transition

The concept of a global energy transition has become a key subject in discussions about the future of the energy sector, with implications that extend beyond national borders and economies. In the face of urgent climate change and environmental sustainability challenges, the need for a fundamental shift in our energy systems is becoming increasingly recognised. This transition involves various changes, such as the gradual phase-out of fossil fuels in favour of renewable and sustainable energy sources, and the adoption of more efficient technologies and practices. This transformation is driven by changing consumer preferences, technological advances, and the need to mitigate the effects of carbon emissions. The global energy transition represents an economic and technological revolution, as well as a profound restructuring of geopolitical power relations. Countries that successfully adapt to and complete this transition will enjoy considerable advantages, while those that depend on traditional energy sources could face economic and strategic challenges. Recognising these issues, many governments and industry leaders are re-evaluating their long-term energy strategies to secure their position in the evolving global energy landscape. The transition also offers opportunities for new collaborations and partnerships, as well as the chance to adopt innovative approaches to energy governance and policy. To ensure the success of this transition, it is crucial to grasp the intricate interplay between energy, the economy, politics, and environmental management. This requires proactive planning, investment in research and development, and a willingness to adopt bold, innovative strategies. Against this backdrop, this chapter explores the multiple dimensions of the global energy transition, examining its impact on the Gulf region and highlighting the strategic imperatives for stakeholders.

The current energy landscape in the Gulf

The Gulf region has long been recognised as a crucial player in the global energy landscape thanks to its abundant hydrocarbon resources, which have underpinned its economic development and strategic importance. Home to some of the world's largest proven oil reserves and significant natural gas deposits, the Gulf states have played a central role in meeting global energy demand for decades. Their central role in oil production and exports gives the region considerable influence over international energy markets, shaping geopolitical dynamics and relationships. Furthermore, its location at the crossroads of major shipping routes further reinforces its importance as an energy hub.

However, the region is not immune to the profound changes currently affecting the global energy sector. The

Gulf's current energy landscape is undergoing upheaval due to technological advances, changing consumer preferences, and efforts to mitigate climate change.

As traditional energy markets change, Gulf monarchies must re-evaluate their energy strategies and diversify their economies to ensure sustainable growth and resilience. Despite their heavy dependence on oil and gas revenues, Gulf states have demonstrated a growing awareness of the need to adapt to the evolving energy landscape.

Investments in renewable energy projects, such as solar and wind power, signal a strategic shift towards sustainability and reducing carbon emissions. Initiatives to improve energy efficiency and develop cleaner technologies are also gaining ground, demonstrating a proactive response to the challenges posed by the global energy transition.

Additionally, Gulf countries are exploring innovative collaboration models with international partners and investors to promote sustainable energy development. Through strategic partnerships and joint ventures, the region aims to leverage its energy production assets while seizing opportunities in emerging renewable energy markets. This approach not only aligns with international efforts to promote clean energy, but also establishes the Gulf region as a pivotal player in the future of the global energy supply.

Faced with the complexity of today's energy landscape, the Gulf region is at a critical juncture requiring informed decision-making and an understanding of evolving dynamics. Although continued demand for hydrocarbons will remain the economic bedrock of the Gulf, the need to adapt to the realities of the global energy transition is redefining priorities and prompting strategic realignment. As the Gulf navigates this phase of transformation, it is seeking to leverage its energy capabilities to promote sustainable development, contribute to the global energy transition, and consolidate its position as a leading energy player in the 21st century.

Drivers of the global energy transition

The global energy landscape is undergoing rapid transformation, driven by several interrelated factors that are reshaping the way we produce and consume energy. One of the main drivers of this transition is the growing awareness of the environmental impact of traditional energy sources, particularly fossil fuels. Concerns about climate change, air pollution, and the unsustainable extraction of resources have prompted international efforts to switch to cleaner, more sustainable energy alternatives. Technological advances in renewable energy production and storage have also made these sources increasingly viable and cost-effective. Falling costs for solar and wind energy, combined with advances in battery technology, have significantly boosted the economic competitiveness of renewable energy. Another key driver of this transition is changing geopolitical dynamics and the quest for energy independence. Countries worldwide are seeking to reduce their reliance on oil and gas imports, thereby enhancing their energy security by sourcing energy domestically or regionally. This quest for energy independence has significant implications for global energy markets and trade. Furthermore, shifting consumer preferences and societal expectations are driving the shift towards cleaner energy sources. As public awareness of environmental issues grows, so does the demand for sustainable and ethically sourced energy. This trend is influencing investment patterns and business strategies, as companies seek to respond to these new expectations. Government policies and regulations also play a crucial role in this transition. Subsidies, incentives, and carbon pricing mechanisms can strongly influence the adoption of renewable energy technologies and the phase-out of fossil fuels. Understanding the interdependence of these forces and their implications for the future of global energy systems is essential in this complex context, particularly in regions such as the Gulf, which have traditionally been heavily dependent on hydrocarbons.

Impact on hydrocarbon-dependent economies

As the global energy transition accelerates, the Gulf region's traditionally hydrocarbon-dependent economies are facing profound and multifaceted impacts. These nations have historically relied on oil and gas revenues to ensure their economic prosperity, but are now forced to navigate a rapidly changing energy landscape marked by increasing diversification and the global integration of renewable energies. The repercussions of this transition are being felt in various aspects of Gulf economies.

One of the most pressing concerns is the potential decline in demand for traditional hydrocarbons. As major consumer markets pursue decarbonisation goals and adopt alternative energy sources, the Gulf's traditional revenue streams are becoming increasingly volatile and uncertain. This shift poses fiscal challenges and requires a strategic reassessment of economic policies and long-term planning.

The implications also extend to investment dynamics, as the appeal of traditional hydrocarbon-related projects may diminish due to growing global interest in sustainable, low-carbon initiatives. This change in investment preferences requires a rethink of how capital is allocated and resources are used in the region. This could lead to innovation and diversification in sectors that have been overshadowed by the dominance of hydrocarbons.

On a broader scale, this transition further emphasises the urgent need for economic diversification in the Gulf states. Recognising the need to reduce their dependence on hydrocarbon revenues, governments are stepping up efforts to foster the development of diversified, knowledge-based economies capable of withstanding shocks linked to energy market fluctuations. Initiatives to encourage entrepreneurship, technological innovation, and industrial diversification are gaining ground, driven by the need to ensure long-term economic resilience and competitiveness.

However, as they embark on this transformative journey, Gulf economies must address the risk of social and labour market disruptions. Given the central role that oil and gas have historically played in employment and public sector financing, skilful navigation of the transition is required to minimise disruption and maximise opportunities in new economic sectors.

In conclusion, the impact of the global energy transition on hydrocarbon-dependent Gulf economies is profound and multifaceted, necessitating a comprehensive reassessment of revenue sources, investment strategies, and economic structures. As the region moves towards sustainability and resilience, leveraging innovation and diversifying the economy becomes essential to ensuring a prosperous future amid changing global energy paradigms.

Economic diversification efforts

The Gulf region has long been recognised for its heavy dependence on hydrocarbon resources, which form the backbone of its economy. However, in response to the evolving global energy landscape and the imperative to mitigate carbon emissions, Gulf countries have intensified their efforts to diversify their economies. These efforts encompass a wide range of initiatives aimed at reducing dependence on oil and natural gas revenues and developing non-oil sectors. These initiatives include short-term measures and long-term strategic planning to create sustainable and resilient economies. The need for economic diversification is based on the recognition that excessive dependence on hydrocarbons poses a significant threat to the region's economic stability and growth prospects. Developing non-oil industries such as tourism, manufacturing, healthcare, education and technology is an essential part of this process. By promoting growth in these sectors, Gulf countries are seeking to create new sources of revenue and employment, thereby reducing their vulnerability to fluctuations in global oil prices. Additionally, economic diversification efforts involve investing in human capital and education to develop a highly skilled and versatile workforce capable of driving innovation in various economic fields. These efforts also involve promoting entrepreneurship and small and medium-sized enterprises (SMEs) to stimulate innovation and foster a dynamic business environment. Fostering a culture of innovation and R&D is also essential for successfully diversifying the Gulf economies. This requires investment in research infrastructure, collaboration with international institutions, and the establishment of regulatory frameworks that encourage innovation. Leveraging strategic partnerships and foreign investment is also essential for accessing new markets and technologies. By forming alliances with global industry leaders and attracting foreign direct investment, Gulf countries can benefit from expertise and resources that are difficult to obtain domestically, thereby accelerating the achievement of their economic diversification goals.

Overall, economic diversification efforts in the Gulf region represent a fundamental rebalancing of economic priorities and a structural transformation towards creating more balanced and sustainable economies. Although challenges remain, the proactive and strategic measures taken by Gulf countries demonstrate their determination to adapt to the changing global energy landscape and ensure the long-term prosperity of their citizens.

Technological innovations and renewable energy

As the global energy landscape shifts towards sustainability and renewable energy sources, the Gulf region must adapt and innovate. Technological advances are playing a key role in this transition. Solar energy, in particular, has become a priority for the Gulf countries thanks to their abundant year-round sunshine. Large-scale solar projects, including concentrated solar power (CSP) and photovoltaic (PV) systems, are being developed at an accelerated pace, establishing Gulf countries as leaders in solar energy. Additionally, advances in wind turbine technology have enabled wind energy to be exploited in certain coastal areas, thereby diversifying the region's energy mix. Alongside these traditional renewable energy sources, exploring innovative technologies such as tidal and geothermal energy could expand the Gulf's capabilities in this area. Integrating energy storage solutions such as batteries into the distribution network and hydrogen production enables the efficient use of intermittent renewable energy sources, ensuring grid stability and reliability. These technological innovations pave the way for a more sustainable energy future and offer economic opportunities in terms of research and manufacturing capabilities. Furthermore, digitalisation and smart grid initiatives facilitate efficient energy management and enhance the integration of renewable energy into existing electricity infrastructure, promoting a resilient energy ecosystem. The Gulf's commitment to technological innovation in renewable energy highlights its strategic need to position itself as a pioneer in the global energy transition while addressing environmental concerns and reducing carbon emissions. As the Gulf embarks on this transformative journey, collaborating with international research institutions and industrial partners is essential in order to acquire the necessary knowledge and expertise, thereby strengthening the region's position as a major contributor to the global advancement of renewable energy.

Policy responses and strategic reorientation

Faced with the global energy transition, Gulf states are adapting their policies to adapt to the changing energy landscape. Recognising the challenges posed by climate change and the growing momentum towards renewable energy, these countries have launched a series of proactive measures aimed at ensuring their long-term sustainability and competitiveness. A key aspect of this reorientation is formulating and implementing comprehensive energy policies that prioritise diversification, innovation, and responsible environmental management. These policies encompass a wide range of initiatives, including developing and implementing renewable energy targets, providing incentives to invest in clean energy and promoting energy efficiency measures in various sectors. Gulf governments are also fostering partnerships with international organisations, technology companies and research institutes, leveraging their expertise and resources to advance renewable energy programmes. This collaborative approach facilitates knowledge transfer and capacity building, fostering the creation of a more dynamic and resilient energy ecosystem in the region.

The strategic shift also involves reforming existing regulatory frameworks and investment incentives to adapt to the changing energy landscape. Gulf states are reviewing their subsidy systems, introducing carbon pricing mechanisms, and adopting regulations that favour renewable energy to create a level playing field for sustainable energy solutions. By aligning economic incentives with environmental goals, these policy adjustments aim to stimulate private-sector participation in renewable energy projects, while also mitigating the environmental impact of traditional energy sources.

This strategic reorientation also extends beyond national policies to include geopolitical and diplomatic commitments centred on regional collaboration and competition. Gulf states are participating in multilateral platforms and initiatives that promote energy cooperation, such as regional grid interconnection, joint research and development projects, and cross-border infrastructure. These collaborative efforts aim to optimise resource use, enhance energy security and foster a more interconnected, resilient energy network across the Gulf region.

At the same time, as the global energy transition intensifies, competition among states for leadership in renewable energy adoption and innovation has also become a central issue for Gulf countries. In order to remain at the forefront of this energy shift, policymakers are positioning their countries strategically as hubs for renewable energy investment, as well as for research and development centres and incubators for sustainable technologies. This competition is driving technological progress, infrastructure development, and investment in human capital, establishing the Gulf as a pivotal player in the global shift towards a low-carbon economy.

The policy responses and strategic reorientations undertaken by Gulf states demonstrate a proactive, multifaceted approach to addressing the challenges and seizing the opportunities of the global energy transition. By embracing renewable energy technologies, fostering regional collaboration, and recalibrating their policy frameworks, these countries are well positioned to navigate the complexities of the energy transition effectively and ensure a sustainable and prosperous future for their societies.

Regional collaboration and competition

As the global energy landscape undergoes a profound transformation, the Gulf region is at a critical juncture where regional collaboration and competition will play a central role in shaping its future. Collaborative initiatives among Gulf countries, such as joint investment projects, infrastructure development, and knowledge-sharing, could strengthen the region's collective resilience and competitiveness in a rapidly changing energy market. Furthermore, leveraging each country's unique strengths and resources through strategic partnerships can promote greater efficiency and sustainability in energy production and distribution. However, amid this context of collaboration, competition among Gulf countries for market share, technological leadership, and influence in the energy market is also intensifying. The race to diversify energy portfolios and build renewable energy capacity is fostering innovation and pushing the boundaries of research and development, while also driving healthy competition. While this spirit of competition can drive progress, it also poses challenges as countries seek to consolidate their position in the evolving global energy hierarchy and compete for market dominance. Moreover, the competitive landscape is further complicated by the overlap of geopolitical dynamics and historical rivalries. Maintaining the delicate balance between cooperation and rivalry requires astute diplomacy and strategic engagement. It is crucial for Gulf countries to have a clear understanding of the broader regional and global implications of these dynamics. In order to create an environment conducive to collaboration and healthy competition, transparent communication must be established, mutual trust must be built and a shared vision for a sustainable energy future must be embraced. Ultimately, the success of regional collaboration and healthy competition depends on the Gulf countries' ability to strike a balance that maximises collective gains while respecting individual aspirations and interests. As the Gulf navigates this balance, the outcomes of regional collaboration and competition will profoundly influence the region's trajectory in the era of the global energy transition, shaping not only economic and energy outcomes, but also broader geopolitical and social dimensions.

Long-term socio-economic implications

As the Gulf region undergoes a transformative global energy transition, it is crucial to recognise the long-term socio-economic implications that will determine its future trajectory. The transition to a low-carbon world presents challenges and opportunities for Gulf states, affecting various aspects of their societies and economies. One of the main areas of concern is the potential for structural changes in the labour market. As hydrocarbon industries become less important, there will be a need to develop new skills and create employment opportunities in emerging sectors such as renewable energy, technology, and sustainable infrastructure. This could also lead to a re-evaluation of education and training programmes, aligning them with evolving labour market demands. Additionally, the transition to cleaner energy sources will necessitate a reevaluation of national economic strategies. Gulf governments will need to adjust their fiscal policies, investment priorities, and trade relations in order to adapt to the evolving energy landscape. Furthermore, there is a growing recognition of the need to promote sustainability and environmental preservation. The transition to renewable energy and carbon neutrality will require significant investment in infrastructure and a reallocation of resources. This will promote the emergence of new industries while potentially leading to the disappearance of traditional ones. This transition also offers Gulf states the opportunity to leverage their strategic geographical location to become hubs for innovation in green technologies and sustainable development initiatives. Another key aspect of the long-term socio-economic implications is the potential for social transformation. The transition to a low-carbon economy could influence urbanisation patterns, lifestyle choices, and cultural norms in the Gulf region. It could encourage further investment in smart cities, green transport, and environmentally friendly consumption practices. This transition could also inspire social entrepreneurship and community engagement in environmental preservation efforts, thereby promoting a more sustainable quality of life. Furthermore, the global energy transition offers

Gulf states the chance to redefine their role on the international stage. By proactively adopting renewable energy and sustainability initiatives, these countries can strengthen their global reputation, attract foreign investment, and contribute positively to international climate programmes. Embracing this transition could enable the Gulf to diversify its diplomatic and economic partnerships, positioning it as a leader in the global effort towards a greener future. In conclusion, the long-term socio-economic implications of the global energy transition for the Gulf are manifold and include changes to labour markets, economic policies, environmental management, social dynamics, and global influence. Adapting to these changes will require proactive planning, innovative thinking, and collaborative action from governments, businesses, and civil society. Successfully navigating these changes will enable the Gulf to establish itself as a resilient and progressive region within the evolving global energy landscape.

Future prospects for the Gulf in a low-carbon world

The transition to a low-carbon world presents challenges and opportunities for the Gulf region. As the global shift towards renewable energy and decarbonisation accelerates, Gulf states are at a critical juncture where they must adapt their economies and energy policies to align with the evolving global landscape.

One of the most promising prospects for the Gulf in a low-carbon world is to leverage its financial resources and strategic positioning to become a major player in the renewable energy sector. With its abundant sunshine and vast desert expanses, the region is ideally placed to harness solar energy on a large scale. Investing in solar infrastructure alongside advances in wind and hydroelectric technologies could establish the Gulf as a clean energy production and export hub, diversifying its economic base beyond traditional fossil fuels.

Additionally, the transition to a low-carbon economy provides Gulf states with an opportunity to lead the way in technological innovation, particularly in carbon capture and storage (CCS), and to develop sustainable oil and gas extraction practices. By actively investing in research and development, the region could reduce its carbon footprint and demonstrate to the world that it cares about the environment.

However, the transition to a low-carbon world will also require significant changes to the region's social and economic fabric. As dependence on oil revenues declines, the region will need to implement strategies to create jobs, promote sustainable urban development, and diversify industry. A successful transition will require investment in education and retraining programmes to equip the workforce with the skills needed for emerging renewable energy and technology sectors.

Furthermore, the region's geopolitical position could change profoundly as global dependence on oil and gas declines. Strategic alliances and diplomatic commitments will need to be adjusted to align with the new energy order.

Collaborative initiatives with other nations and regions, as well as proactive participation in international climate agreements, could strengthen the Gulf's position as a responsible and visionary global partner in the quest for environmental sustainability. Ultimately, Gulf policymakers must demonstrate visionary leadership and make proactive decisions to envision a future in a low-carbon world.

By strategically leveraging renewable energy, encouraging innovation, valuing human capital and adapting to changing geopolitical realities, the Gulf could play a lasting and influential role in shaping the global energy landscape for generations to come.

7

Environmental Challenges
Climate Change and Sustainable Futures

Introduction to Environmental Issues in the Gulf Region

The Gulf region faces unique environmental challenges resulting from a combination of natural factors and human activities. Understanding and addressing these challenges is essential because of their significant implications for the region's ecosystems, economies and societies. The region's unique geographical characteristics, including its arid climate, make it particularly vulnerable to threats such as water scarcity, desertification, and extreme weather events. Dependence on hydrocarbon resources for economic development has also had significant environmental impacts, including air and water pollution, habitat destruction, and greenhouse gas emissions. Rapid urbanisation and population growth in Gulf countries further exacerbate these challenges by placing additional pressure on natural resources and contributing to soil degradation. Recognising and comprehensively addressing these issues is essential in order to develop effective strategies for sustainable development and environmental preservation in the region. Furthermore, as the international community recognises the urgency of climate change, the Gulf region is at the forefront of environmental vulnerability and resilience. Therefore, improving our understanding of the region's environmental issues would benefit not only the Gulf states, but also provide valuable insights for the broader debate on climate action and sustainability. In the following sections, we will analyse the specific environmental issues facing the Gulf in detail, exploring their root causes and impacts, and proposing ways to promote a more sustainable and resilient future for the region.

Analysis of Climate Change Impacts on Regional Ecosystems

Climate change poses significant challenges to the fragile ecosystems of the Gulf region. Rising temperatures, changing rainfall patterns, and extreme weather events are disrupting the balance of regional flora and fauna.

The impact of climate change on coastal and marine ecosystems is particularly concerning, as rising sea levels threaten habitats and biodiversity. Additionally, warming Gulf waters are causing coral bleaching, endangering marine species that depend on these complex ecosystems. Furthermore, desertification and loss of vegetation are exacerbating soil erosion and degrading landscapes in the region's arid areas. The decline of native plant species and changes in wildlife migration patterns are evidence of the profound impact of climate change on regional ecosystems. These ecological changes have a knock-on effect on the livelihoods of communities that depend on natural resources, as well as on economic activities that rely on ecosystem services, such as agriculture, fishing and tourism. Furthermore, disturbances to ecosystems have implications for human health, as changes in vector distribution favour the spread of infectious diseases.

In response to these challenges, efforts are being made to understand and mitigate the impact of climate change on regional ecosystems. Scientists and researchers are monitoring ecological changes and conducting studies to assess the vulnerability and resilience of various species and habitats. Conservation initiatives aimed at preserving key ecosystems and biodiversity-rich areas are being developed, focusing on protected area management and restoration projects. Collaborative research and data-sharing mechanisms are improving our understanding of the complex interactions between climate change and regional ecosystems. Furthermore, indigenous knowledge and practices are being incorporated into adaptation strategies to bolster ecosystem resilience.

The role of policy and governance in addressing the impacts of climate change on ecosystems is crucial. Integrated approaches that align national environmental strategies with international commitments, such as the Paris Agreement, are essential to ensure concerted action. This requires robust regulatory frameworks, cross-sectoral coordination, and innovative financing mechanisms to support ecosystem conservation and climate change adaptation measures. Furthermore, raising public awareness and engaging communities is vital to encourage responsibility towards regional ecosystems and promote sustainable practices.

In conclusion, analysing the impacts of climate change on regional ecosystems highlights the urgent need for proactive measures to preserve the Gulf region's ecological integrity. By understanding and addressing these impacts, stakeholders can work towards building resilient and sustainable ecosystems that can withstand the challenges posed by a changing climate.

Water scarcity and management strategies

Water scarcity is a major challenge in this region, where arid and semi-arid conditions are exacerbated by the scarcity of freshwater resources. The relentless growth of urban centres and the increasing demand for agricultural resources puts further pressure on available water. With rainfall expected to decline and traditional water sources potentially being disrupted by climate change, tackling water scarcity has become a top priority for Gulf countries. Comprehensive management strategies are essential to address this. Adopting innovative technologies for water desalination and treatment is a crucial aspect of this. Desalination plants already play a vital role in alleviating water scarcity by providing drinking water from plentiful seawater. However, the increased use of desalination requires us to critically assess its environmental and economic viability. Investment in research and development is imperative to improve the efficiency of desalination and minimise its environmental impact. Promoting water conservation practices at individual and industrial levels is also essential to reduce excessive water consumption. Essential elements of a multidimensional approach to water resource conservation include the implementation of advanced irrigation technologies in agriculture, the enforcement of regulations for efficient water use in industries, and public awareness of responsible water consumption. Integrated water management plans that incorporate water reuse, rainwater harvesting, and groundwater recharge will also contribute to sustainable water management. Collaborative efforts among Gulf countries regarding transboundary water management and the sharing of best practices and efficient use of shared water resources are essential to finding long-term solutions. Furthermore, improving wastewater treatment and reuse infrastructure can mitigate the impact of water scarcity. This strategy addresses the challenge of water scarcity while preserving the environment by reducing pollution and protecting ecosystems. It is also crucial to consider water scarcity in urban planning and development to ensure that cities are designed and expanded in a way that promotes sustainable water use. Policy frameworks focused on pricing mechanisms, efficiency standards and regulatory measures play a central role in shaping water usage behaviours and practices. Ultimately, addressing water scarcity requires concerted efforts from the public and private sectors, as well as civil society. By adopting a holistic approach that integrates advanced technologies and promotes international collaboration, the Gulf region can overcome water scarcity challenges and transition to a more sustainable water future.

Air quality and urban pollution: challenges and responses

Urban areas in the Gulf region have experienced significant economic growth and development in recent years, leading to increased industrialisation, urbanisation, and population density. While these trends have brought many benefits, they have also led to a worrying increase in air pollution levels and a deterioration in air quality. Urban pollution poses serious risks to health and the environment, with repercussions for the well-being of the population and the sustainability of the natural environment.

Exploring the complex issues related to air quality and urban pollution in the Gulf region, as well as potential solutions to mitigate these challenges is a significant step. Understanding the sources of urban pollution is crucial. These include various human activities, such as vehicle emissions, industrial processes, construction activities and energy production. These activities release pollutants such as fine particulate matter, nitrogen oxides, sulphur dioxide, volatile organic compounds and carbon monoxide into the atmosphere, contributing to air pollution and associated health risks. Furthermore, rapid urbanisation has led to increased energy consumption, resulting in higher emissions from electricity generation and transport and exacerbating air quality concerns. Poor air quality can have a profound effect on health, causing respiratory diseases, cardiovascular disorders and other chronic conditions. Vulnerable populations, including children, the elderly, and individuals with pre-existing health conditions, are particularly at risk. To combat urban pollution, a comprehensive approach integrating regulatory measures, technological advances, public awareness campaigns and international cooperation is needed. Regulatory frameworks that focus on emission standards, vehicle inspections and industrial pollution control play a crucial role in reducing pollution levels. Investing in cleaner, more sustainable transport options, such as electric vehicles and public transport networks, can significantly reduce emissions and improve air quality. Promoting energy efficiency and renewable energy sources can help to reduce urban pollution and decrease dependence on fossil fuels. Additionally, urban planning and development strategies that prioritise green spaces, pedestrian infrastructure, and sustainable construction practices can reduce air pollution and enhance the quality of life in cities. Public engagement and education are essential components of any intervention strategy as they encourage community participation and behavioural changes that contribute to protecting air quality. Finally, given the transboundary nature of air pollution, international collaboration and knowledge sharing on best practices in air quality management are essential. By implementing these measures and preserving air quality, the Gulf region can create healthier and more sustainable urban environments for current and future generations.

Renewable energy initiatives: progress and potential

These initiatives have attracted considerable interest in recent years, reflecting a growing awareness of the need to diversify energy sources and reduce dependence on fossil fuels. Progress in integrating renewable energy into the region's energy mix demonstrates the potential for sustainable development and environmental management. A major advance has been the widespread adoption of solar technologies, which harness clean energy from the region's abundant sunshine. Large-scale solar projects, such as concentrated solar power (CSP) and photovoltaic (PV) systems, have strengthened solar energy's position as a viable alternative to traditional electricity generation methods. Additionally, wind power projects, particularly in coastal areas, have shown promise in diversifying the renewable energy supply. Exploring offshore wind farms could significantly enhance the region's capacity to generate renewable energy. Furthermore, initiatives to promote energy efficiency and conservation have played a pivotal role in developing renewable energy sources. Technological advances, particularly in large-scale battery systems, have facilitated the effective integration of intermittent renewable resources into the existing electricity grid, thereby improving reliability and resilience. Investments in research and development have also stimulated innovation in renewable energy, promoting cutting-edge solutions and strengthening the competitiveness of sustainable technologies. Collaboration with international partners and the involvement of private sector actors has catalysed progress in renewable energy initiatives, creating new opportunities for investment and technology exchange. The Gulf's renewable energy potential exceeds domestic consumption, offering opportunities for regional exports and cross-border project collaboration. As momentum for renewable energy continues to build, policymakers and industry leaders recognise the strategic importance of transitioning to a more sustainable, diversified energy landscape. This transformative trajectory highlights renewable energy's considerable potential to mitigate environmental challenges, stimulate economic growth, enhance energy security, and foster innovation.

Biodiversity Conservation: Preserving Natural Heritage

Biodiversity conservation is an essential aspect of preserving the Gulf region's natural heritage. The region's unique and diverse ecosystems, ranging from coastal areas to deserts, are home to rich fauna and flora that contribute to the region's ecological balance and cultural identity. However, rapid urbanisation, industrial development and human activities pose significant threats to these fragile ecosystems, leading to habitat loss, degradation and biodiversity decline. Therefore, it is crucial that stakeholders, including government agencies, non-governmental organisations and local communities, prioritise implementing effective conservation measures to protect the region's precious natural heritage. One essential approach to conserving vital habitats is identifying and protecting key biodiversity areas, such as wetlands, mangroves and marine reserves. Additionally, establishing protected areas and nature reserves helps preserve the genetic diversity of plant and animal species, ensuring their survival for future generations. Furthermore, raising public awareness of the importance of biodiversity and its direct link to human well-being can foster a sense of responsibility and encourage the population to manage resources responsibly. Collaborative research efforts are essential for assessing the status of different species and ecosystems, monitoring population trends, and understanding the impact of human interventions on local biodiversity. Integrating traditional ecological knowledge into modern conservation practices enhances the effectiveness of initiatives by leveraging indigenous knowledge to sustainably manage natural resources. International partnerships and agreements for biodiversity conservation can facilitate knowledge exchange, build capacity and encourage collective action to address cross-border conservation challenges. By adopting sustainable practices and integrating biodiversity considerations into various development policies and plans, Gulf states can preserve their natural heritage while promoting economic growth and social well-being. Ultimately, biodiversity conservation is a moral and strategic imperative, investing in the resilience and sustainability of the Gulf region's ecosystems and being a responsibility that transcends borders and generations.

Waste management and resource efficiency

Waste management and resource efficiency are essential elements of sustainable development in this region. As rapid economic growth and urbanisation put increasing pressure on natural resources and generate ever-growing volumes of waste, comprehensive and effective waste management strategies must be adopted. Current waste disposal practices in many Gulf countries, including open dumping and landfilling, pose significant risks to the environment and public health.

There is therefore an urgent need to transition to more sustainable approaches that prioritise reduction, reuse, and recycling. Improving waste management requires efforts in both the municipal and industrial sectors. Municipal waste, including household, commercial and institutional waste, poses a significant challenge due to its diverse composition and large quantity.

Implementing source separation programmes, promoting composting and improving recycling infrastructure can significantly reduce the amount of municipal waste sent to landfills. Introducing advanced waste-to-energy technologies can help exploit the energy contained in organic and combustible waste while enabling the production of renewable energy and reducing the burden on landfills.

In the industrial sector, the focus should be on reducing production waste, optimising material use, and implementing environmentally friendly manufacturing processes. Industrial symbiosis, whereby waste or by-products from one industry are used as raw materials by another, is an innovative approach to improving resource efficiency and reducing waste. Encouraging industries to adhere to the principles of the circular economy, such as the cradle-to-cradle approach or extending product lifetimes, can foster a paradigm shift towards a sustainable, resource-efficient economy.

Integrated approaches to resource efficiency also play a key role in reducing the environmental footprint of economic activities. These approaches involve adopting cleaner production techniques, optimising water and energy use, and reducing raw material consumption. Furthermore, encouraging investment in sustainable technologies and providing financial incentives to companies that adopt resource-efficient practices can drive profound transformation across all sectors.

Collaboration among stakeholders is essential to advancing waste management and resource efficiency programmes. Governments, the private sector, academic institutions, and civil society organisations must collaborate to develop and implement comprehensive policies, regulations, and initiatives. Public awareness campaigns and educational programmes can foster a culture of responsible resource consumption, waste sorting, and sustainable lifestyle choices among residents.

By integrating waste management and resource efficiency into the broader framework of sustainable development, the Gulf region can mitigate environmental degradation, preserve valuable resources, and establish the foundations for a resilient and prosperous future.

Green buildings and sustainable urban development

As the region experiences rapid urbanisation and population growth, the demand for infrastructure and buildings continues to rise. Indeed, the construction and operation of buildings contributes significantly to energy consumption, resource depletion and greenhouse gas emissions. Therefore, it is imperative to integrate the principles of green building and sustainable urban development to create environmentally friendly and resilient cities in the Gulf region. Green building practices take a holistic approach covering design, construction, operation and demolition, aiming to minimise environmental impact while maximising resource efficiency. This involves using energy-efficient technologies, adopting sustainable materials, optimising water consumption and reducing waste production throughout a building's life cycle. Furthermore, sustainable urban development focuses not only on individual structures, but also on the urban fabric as a whole, including urban planning, transport systems, public spaces and community participation. It emphasises creating mixed-use, pedestrian-friendly neighbourhoods; promoting public transport; improving green spaces; and fostering social inclusion. Adopting green construction methods and sustainable urban development strategies reduces the ecological footprint of cities and improves the quality of life of their inhabitants. Introducing architectural designs that prioritise natural lighting, ventilation and thermal comfort enables buildings to reduce their dependence on mechanical systems and lower their energy consumption and operating costs. Additionally, integrating renewable energy technologies such as solar panels and wind turbines into urban landscapes promotes self-sufficiency and resilience in the face of energy challenges. Moreover, sustainable urban development strategies such as compact urban planning and green infrastructure can mitigate the impact of urban heat islands, enhance air quality and protect biodiversity. These initiatives mitigate environmental impact and stimulate economic growth, creating jobs and attracting foreign investment. However, transitioning to green construction and sustainable urban development requires strong political will, effective governance, and collaboration between stakeholders. This involves harmonising regulatory frameworks, updating building codes, and introducing financial mechanisms and accreditation programmes to encourage private sector participation. International cooperation and knowledge exchange with global sustainability leaders could provide the Gulf region with valuable insights and best practices. Therefore, integrating green construction and sustainable urban development is essential to shaping the region's urban landscape of the future, promoting responsible environmental management and cultivating prosperous, inclusive communities.

Policy frameworks and international cooperation

In the context of environmental challenges such as climate change, the importance of policy frameworks and international cooperation cannot be overstated. Gulf countries must recognise the interconnectedness of environmental issues and the necessity of collaborative action on a global scale. Now, let's examine the different aspects of policy frameworks and the need for international cooperation to foster a sustainable future.

Policy frameworks form the backbone of any environmental strategy, guiding legislative measures, regulatory mechanisms, and institutional structures. In the Gulf region, each country has developed its own policies to address environmental concerns. However, there is a collective awareness that a harmonised approach is essential to effectively address cross-border issues. This involves aligning national policies with international conventions and agreements to promote a coherent and synergistic response to shared challenges.

International cooperation plays a central role in environmental policymaking in the Gulf region. Collaborative initiatives with international organisations, neighbouring countries, and global initiatives facilitate knowledge sharing, capacity building, and technology transfer. Joint research projects, exchange programmes and cross-border partnerships improve understanding of regional environmental dynamics and facilitate the adoption of best practices. Multilateral commitments also enable Gulf states to leverage global expertise and resources to develop innovative solutions and mitigate environmental risks.

Fostering international environmental cooperation requires the establishment of strong diplomatic relations. Bilateral and multilateral dialogues provide platforms for engagement, negotiation and consensus building. By forming strategic alliances and partnerships, Gulf countries can amplify their collective voice on environmental issues in international forums, thereby influencing global discourse and policymaking. Advocacy efforts and coalition building strengthen the region's position as a responsible actor in the global environmental governance landscape.

Integrating environmental considerations into broader international agendas, such as those relating to trade, energy, and security, is also essential to ensuring a holistic approach to sustainable development. Gulf countries must actively participate in diplomatic negotiations and international summits to demonstrate their dedication to environmental management and establish alliances that support their long-term sustainability objectives.

In conclusion, robust policy frameworks and proactive participation in international cooperation are vital for steering the Gulf region towards a sustainable future. By taking on their shared responsibilities, leveraging their collective expertise and forming meaningful partnerships, Gulf countries can address environmental challenges and contribute to the global quest for ecological resilience and sustainable development.

Pathways to a sustainable future: strategic recommendations

When considering the path towards a sustainable future for the Gulf region, it is crucial to build upon the policy frameworks and international cooperation strategies outlined in the previous section. Strategic recommendations should align with global sustainability goals while taking into account the Gulf region's unique environmental characteristics. Firstly, adopting renewable energy sources and prioritising investment in clean energy technologies will be essential. This transition could reduce carbon emissions, enhance energy security, and diversify economies. Collaboration between Gulf countries and their international partners can facilitate the exchange of expertise and technology, foster innovation, and accelerate the adoption of sustainable energy solutions. Additionally, comprehensive water management strategies are crucial for combatting water scarcity and ensuring the sustainable use of water resources. This includes the use of advanced irrigation techniques, desalination technologies, and conservation measures to optimise water use across all sectors. Furthermore, improving waste management systems and promoting circular economies will reduce environmental impact and optimise resource use. Integrating waste-to-energy processes, recycling initiatives and sustainable production practices will enable the region to reduce its ecological footprint and transition to a more sustainable model of resource utilisation. Additionally, conserving biodiversity through protected areas and habitat restoration projects is crucial for preserving the Gulf's natural heritage. Governments and stakeholders must collaborate to establish and enforce regulations that protect biodiversity-rich areas and mitigate habitat degradation. Adopting green building practices and sustainable urban development is also essential for building a sustainable future. Designing infrastructure that prioritises energy efficiency, uses environmentally friendly materials, and incorporates green spaces can promote resilience and improve the quality of life in urban environments. Finally, promoting knowledge sharing and capacity building through educational programmes, research initiatives and public awareness campaigns is essential for the success of this transformation. These efforts will enable communities, policymakers and businesses to contribute to, and benefit from, sustainable development. By taking concerted action and committing to these strategic recommendations, the Gulf region can pave the way for a sustainable future that balances economic growth with responsible environmental management, ensuring a dynamic and resilient future for generations to come.

Socio-Political Dynamics
National Identity and Popular Sentiment

National identity and popular sentiment

The Gulf countries have long been characterised by complex socio-political dynamics that shape the collective identity and sentiment of their populations. This region, which is rich in history and cultural heritage, has seen the interaction of various factors that influence national identity and popular sentiment. At the heart of these dynamics lie the relationships between tradition and modernity, religion and secularism, and indigenous and external influences. Understanding these nuances is essential to grasping the social fabric of the region. As we delve deeper into our exploration, it becomes clear that the socio-political landscape of these countries is multifaceted. It encompasses elements such as historical heritage, demographic diversity, economic disparities and evolving political structures. These variables intertwine to form the complex social fabric, influencing how individuals identify themselves and define their roles within the wider national society. The geopolitical position of the Gulf countries and their interactions with global forces have also shaped their socio-political environment. The influence of international relations, trade, and strategic alliances has undoubtedly left an indelible mark on the region's collective consciousness. Exploring the themes of identity and sentiment in greater depth is imperative in order to recognise the impact of generational changes and evolving social norms. The intergenerational transmission of cultural values, combined with the rapid pace of social change, creates a dynamic landscape in which traditional and contemporary elements coexist. Alongside this, the role of education, the media, and communication technologies in shaping and disseminating socio-political narratives is crucial. These mechanisms play a central role in constructing and disseminating national narratives and collective sentiments. Our aim is to analyse the multiple facets of the socio-political dynamics of the Gulf countries, outlining the fundamental elements on which national identity and public opinion are based.

Defining National Identity in the Gulf countries

National identity in the Gulf countries is multifaceted and complex, shaped by historical, cultural, and socio-political factors. At the heart of this identity are the shared values, beliefs, traditions and symbols that unite individuals within a given nation and differentiate them from others. In the Gulf context, the notion of national identity has been profoundly influenced by the region's historical heritage, rapid modernisation, economic prosperity, and its diverse demographic composition. Defining national identity in the Gulf countries is an ongoing process reflecting the interaction between tradition and progress, indigenous customs and global influences, and the population's aspirations. The concept of national identity is closely linked to narratives of nationhood and sovereignty, which have evolved in response to internal and external dynamics. Furthermore, the Gulf countries' transition to independence and subsequent attempts to develop cohesive and inclusive national identities have been pivotal in shaping their developmental trajectory. National identity in this region encompasses the collective memory of its inhabitants, including historical experiences, social values and cultural expressions that foster a sense of belonging and unity. The distinctive characteristics of national identity in Gulf countries are reflected in various aspects of public life, including language, religious practices, traditional arts, cuisine, and clothing. These aspects serve as markers for individual and collective identification. The evolving nature of national identity in the Gulf is also evident in current debates and dialogues concerning citizenship, inclusion and social cohesion. As Gulf societies undergo rapid transformation, the discourse on national identity is becoming increasingly nuanced, incorporating diverse perspectives and taking into account contemporary global realities. Consequently, defining and preserving national identity in Gulf countries is a dynamic process requiring careful consideration of historical heritage, cultural pluralism, and future aspirations.

The historical evolution of cultural narratives

The historical evolution of cultural narratives in this region is a fascinating mosaic reflecting the interaction between tradition, modernity, and external influences. The cultural landscape has been shaped by centuries of diverse influences, including trade routes, migratory movements, and geopolitical dynamics. From the early civilisations of Mesopotamia and the great Persian empires, through the spread of Islam, to the subsequent waves of globalisation, each era has left an indelible mark on the cultural fabric of the Gulf.

Ancient myths, folklore, and oral traditions have played a vital role in shaping the collective memory and identity of the region's societies. These cultural narratives serve as a vital link to the past and provide valuable insights into the region's people and their values, beliefs and aspirations. As the Gulf transitioned from nomadic tribal societies to modern nation-states, a rich tapestry of cultural expressions emerged in areas such as literature, architecture, music and the arts, reflecting the region's diverse heritage.

The impact of colonialism and the subsequent quest for independence has also significantly influenced these nations' cultural narratives. Encountering European powers and subsequent nation-building processes sparked debates about the authenticity, preservation and adaptation of traditional practices in the face of modernisation. The tension between preserving cultural heritage and embracing innovation continues to shape the region's contemporary cultural identity.

Furthermore, the discovery of oil wealth and the rapid urbanisation that followed have led to profound societal transformations, including changes in lifestyles, values, and social structures.

These changes have sparked discussions about preserving authentic cultural heritage in the face of global consumer culture and technological advances. The intertwining of cultural narratives with political movements and regional dynamics has further enriched the mosaic of Gulf societies.

Whether through promoting national folklore as a unifying and pride-inspiring tool or reviving traditional crafts as a means of economic empowerment, cultural narratives continue to play a central role in shaping the identities and senses of belonging of Gulf populations.

In conclusion, the historical evolution of cultural narratives in the Gulf countries testifies to the resilience, adaptability, and rich heritage of their populations. Understanding this complex tapestry is crucial for appreciating the nuances of the socio-political dynamics and national identity of this region.

The role of religion and tradition

Religion and tradition play a vital part in shaping the

socio-political dynamics and national identity of Gulf countries. The intertwining of religion with social norms and traditions has been a defining feature for generations, influencing various aspects of daily life, governance, and cultural expression. In the Gulf region, Islam plays a central role in guiding personal conduct, legal systems and community interactions, thereby exerting a tangible influence on the collective consciousness of the population.

Furthermore, the traditional customs and practices that prevail in the Gulf states often have their origins in a long-standing historical heritage, thereby reinforcing the unique identity of each nation. These customs preserve cultural heritage and help forge an identity that distinguishes the Gulf from other regions. Preserving traditions is essential for developing a sense of belonging and continuity, and instils pride and respect for ancestral practices in the region's citizens.

In contemporary society, however, the intersection between religion, tradition, and modernity raises challenging questions about adaptation and preservation. Rapid technological advances and increasing globalisation pose new challenges to traditional ways of life. Gulf societies are constantly striving to strike a delicate balance between respecting religious and traditional values, and accepting progress and development. Additionally, discussions about the evolving roles of men and women within traditional gender norms and religious principles have sparked debates concerning aspirations for equality and social cohesion.

The influence of religion and tradition extends beyond

individual beliefs to the realm of governance and policymaking. Islamic principles exert considerable influence on legal frameworks and ethical considerations, reflecting the deep connection between religion and legislative issues. Furthermore, government entities' promotion of cultural festivals, historical sites, and traditional art forms highlights the recognition of tradition as a strategic asset for national identity and global representation.

Despite the important role of religion and tradition, the dynamism of Gulf societies requires a nuanced approach to navigating a constantly evolving landscape. Balancing heritage preservation with acceptance of progress requires a delicate approach combining introspection and adaptability to foster an environment where the rich tapestry of traditions is respected and an inclusive, forward-looking society is encouraged.

The impact of globalisation on local identities

Globalisation, with its interconnected network of trade, technology, and cultural exchange, has significantly impacted local identities in Gulf countries. This phenomenon has brought about a multitude of changes in various areas of society, particularly in economic, social and cultural spheres. Economically, the influx of multinational companies and integration into global markets has reshaped these countries' traditional economic structures. The transition from an agrarian economy to a service-based economy, coupled with the adoption of Western business practices, has influenced the nature of work and employment dynamics, thereby altering the social fabric. Furthermore, exposure to international consumer trends and lifestyles has led to a redefinition of personal aspirations and consumption patterns among the population, reflecting the impact of globalisation on the daily lives of Gulf residents. On a social and cultural level, the rise of mass media and digital technologies has facilitated the spread of global cultures and ideologies, creating opportunities as well as challenges for local identities. The influence of Western media, entertainment, and fashion has contributed to the blending and hybridisation of cultural norms, challenging traditional value systems and modes of personal expression. Concurrently, this influx of external influences has sparked debates about heritage preservation and cultural authenticity, prompting individuals to reconsider their sense of belonging and identity in an ever-changing global context. Globalisation has also accentuated the Gulf countries' interconnectedness with the rest of the world, fostering intercultural interactions and the exchange of ideas. This has led to a new openness and greater receptivity to diverse perspectives, resulting in a redefinition of community identities and shared values. Consequently, the impact of globalisation on local identities in the Gulf goes beyond simple adaptation to encompass a broader discourse on the reconfiguration and representation of individual and collective identities in a globalised world.

The perspectives and aspirations of young people

The perspectives and aspirations of young people in the Gulf region are exceptionally diverse and dynamic, reflecting a generation navigating between tradition and modernity, and local and global influences. Exposed increasingly to international trends and advances, young people in Gulf countries are developing a unique worldview that combines an appreciation of their heritage with a desire for innovation. This dichotomy results in multiple aspirations, ranging from traditional careers in fields such as medicine, engineering, and public service, to a growing interest in entrepreneurship, technology, and the creative arts.

Furthermore, young people in the Gulf aspire to play a proactive role in developing their communities and countries. Many seek to contribute meaningfully to social progress, aspiring to bring about change through civic engagement, advocacy, and leadership in various fields. Adopting a global perspective, they are keen to participate in international debates, intercultural exchanges, and initiatives that foster global collaboration.

However, despite these optimistic outlooks, young people also face challenges and obstacles that can hinder the realisation of their aspirations. These can include societal expectations, economic uncertainty, and a lack of platforms for expression and participation. Consequently, many young people are striving to make their voices heard and assert their agency by advocating for more inclusive dialogue platforms and working to transform traditional narratives and social structures to align them with contemporary norms.

Furthermore, the perspectives and aspirations of young people in the Gulf region are shaped by their experiences of education and technology, and their exposure to different cultures. Investing in quality education and developing skills has become a fundamental aspiration for those who wish to pursue higher education and gain expertise in specialised fields. At the same time, ubiquitous digital connectivity has sparked a desire to use technology to drive positive change, leading to growing interest in fields related to digital innovation, cybersecurity, and sustainable development.

In conclusion, a comprehensive understanding of the aspirations and perspectives of young people in the Gulf region is essential to envisioning the future trajectory of Gulf societies. By recognising and valuing the diversity of young people's aspirations, policymakers can foster dynamic, inclusive, and forward-looking communities that are capable of navigating the complexities of the contemporary era while preserving their cultural heritage.

Social movements and political reforms

Social movements and political reforms have played an important role in transforming the socio-political landscape of the Gulf region. Over the years, various social groups and local organisations have emerged to advocate for change and address urgent issues in their respective countries.

These movements have sought to address a wide range of concerns, including political representation, human rights, women's empowerment, labour rights and democratic reforms. The dynamics of these movements are influenced by both internal and external factors, including global events, transnational networks, and technological advances.

In recent years, there has been a notable increase in activism and mobilisation among various segments of society, particularly young people. They have used social media and digital technologies to connect, organise, and amplify their voices, raising awareness and encouraging participation in socio-political discourse. The emergence of these movements reflects a desire for stronger civic engagement and an innovative approach to addressing societal challenges.

At the same time, Gulf governments have also introduced initiatives to promote political reform and modernisation. Several Gulf countries are making evident efforts to improve governance structures, increase political participation, and expand civil liberties. These reforms demonstrate an understanding of the evolving socio-political landscape and a commitment to responding to the evolving aspirations of the population.

However, implementing reforms and managing societal demands poses a complex challenge for governments in the region. This requires striking a balance between the need for stability and security, and calls for greater political openness and inclusion, which necessitates a delicate and nuanced approach. The success of political reforms hinges on encouraging dialogue, building trust between state institutions and civil society, and implementing measures that guarantee fundamental rights and freedoms.

Furthermore, the interaction between social movements, government policies and external influences shapes the trajectory of political reforms in the Gulf region. Understanding the motivations, grievances, and aspirations of social actors is essential for developing inclusive and sustainable reform programmes. It is also crucial to foster an environment that encourages constructive participation and pluralism in order to advance the socio-political landscape while maintaining stability and cohesion.

In conclusion, social movements and political reforms in the Gulf region are an ongoing process of social evolution and governmental adaptation. Accepting the dynamics of social change, recognising the diversity of viewpoints and establishing responsive, inclusive mechanisms to foster political engagement are all essential to shaping the future of governance and citizenship in the region.

Media, communication and public perception

In the Gulf region, the media landscape plays a crucial role in shaping public perceptions and influencing societal attitudes. As technology advances, traditional media such as newspapers, television and radio are coexisting with the rapid expansion of digital platforms, including social media and online news portals. Media diversity is an essential channel for disseminating information, reflecting societal discourse and fostering public debate. However, the proliferation of media sources also raises important questions about accuracy, bias and ethical standards. Journalistic integrity and media transparency are vital for enabling citizens to make informed decisions and for fostering constructive dialogue within Gulf societies. Furthermore, the influence of state-controlled media alongside independent voices further complicates the media landscape. Recognising this, Gulf governments are striving to strike a balance between preserving cultural heritage and embracing modernisation. Public perception is closely linked to the representation of national identity, and the media plays a significant role in shaping it. The portrayal of cultural traditions, historical narratives, and contemporary accomplishments significantly influences how the public perceives Gulf countries. Consequently, media strategies often aim to highlight the coexistence of tradition and progress, leveraging technological advances to showcase cultural richness while promoting innovation and development. Initiatives that promote cultural preservation, artistic expression, and an appreciation of heritage through digital platforms are particularly effective in projecting a comprehensive image of the Gulf's evolution. In an increasingly interconnected world, effective communication strategies play a central role in geopolitics, economic diplomacy, and cultural exchange. Maintaining an authentic and nuanced discourse that resonates with local populations and international observers is essential. Navigating this complex terrain requires striking a delicate balance between preserving authenticity and embracing adaptation. As the Gulf's socio-political landscape undergoes transformation, the power of the media to shape perceptions and bridge social divides demands a thoughtful approach that harmonises tradition and progress, heritage and modernity, and authenticity and innovation.

The challenge lies in balancing modernisation and heritage preservation

The Gulf region is at a critical juncture where the forces of modernisation and the need to preserve heritage intersect, presenting a complex challenge for its societies. The rapid pace of economic development and technological progress has brought significant changes to the cultural landscape of Gulf countries. While there is a growing focus on progress and innovation, there is also a growing recognition of the need to preserve the rich heritage, traditions, and cultural practices that have defined these societies for centuries. Reconciliating modernisation and heritage preservation requires a nuanced approach that respects the past while embracing the future.

In the face of rapid modernisation, heritage preservation requires a multifaceted strategy that encompasses various areas of social life. Architectural conservation, for instance, helps maintain the authenticity of historic sites and traditional urban areas, providing a tangible link to the past amidst skyscrapers and futuristic cityscapes. Cultural institutions and museums also play a vital role in safeguarding and promoting the region's art, crafts, and folklore, enabling current and future generations to reconnect with their roots.

Furthermore, language and literature are powerful vehicles for preserving cultural heritage. Efforts to revitalise and promote indigenous languages, dialects, and oral traditions are essential for maintaining the cultural fabric of Gulf societies. This involves investing in educational initiatives that focus on heritage languages, as well as supporting literary works that reflect the region's history and identity.

At the same time, preserving intangible heritage, such as music, dance and traditional rituals, enriches the social fabric and strengthens the pride and identity of Gulf communities. Initiatives to document and safeguard these practices, as well as supporting artisans and artists, are vital for ensuring the continued existence of these invaluable cultural expressions.

While global trends are appealing, Gulf societies must strike a balance between modernity and tradition, leveraging technology and innovation to preserve and promote their unique heritage. Adopting sustainable development practices and integrating traditional knowledge systems into contemporary solutions can facilitate the harmonious coexistence of progress and heritage. By fostering an environment that honours the past while innovating for the future, Gulf societies can successfully navigate the complexities of modernisation while preserving the essence of their cultural heritage.

Conclusion: The future trajectories of Gulf societies

As Gulf societies navigate the path between modernisation and heritage preservation, defining the future trajectories that will shape their cultural, social, and political landscapes becomes imperative. The gradual transformation of Gulf nations is characterised by an evident tension between preserving traditional values and adopting modern ideologies. This dichotomy fuels an ongoing debate about how heritage adapts to rapid globalisation. Recognising the importance of this unprecedented juncture, this analysis concludes by highlighting a few essential trajectories for Gulf societies.

Firstly, the path towards social cohesion and inclusion is proving crucial. The diversity of cultural narratives requires the implementation of inclusive policies that honour and integrate the various ethnicities, beliefs, and traditions within these thriving societies. Acceptance of diversity fosters a sense of national unity and strengthens the social fabric, enabling societies to address the challenges of rapid modernisation.

Additionally, progressive governance and socio-political reforms are essential for the sustainable development of these societies. Alongside modernisation, developing and implementing equitable laws, encouraging political participation, and protecting human rights are vital to ensuring the cohesive integration of tradition and progress. By fostering an environment conducive to dialogue and reform, Gulf countries can realise their potential as global players while preserving the essence of their unique heritage.

Another important step is to use technological advances and innovation to preserve cultural heritage. Striking a balance between tradition and modernity requires innovative methods to preserve and disseminate heritage. Technology provides opportunities to archive, disseminate, and revitalise traditional practices, thereby ensuring their continued relevance in the contemporary era.

In addition, environmental management and sustainability are crucial issues for the future of Gulf societies. Given their rapid modernisation, Gulf countries must proactively address environmental challenges and promote sustainable practices to preserve their natural landscapes and mitigate the adverse effects of climate change. By preserving their environmental awareness while maintaining their unique cultural traditions, Gulf societies can ensure a sustainable future for generations to come.

In summary, the future of Gulf societies depends on their ability to harmonise ancestral customs with the imperatives of progress. This can be achieved by establishing inclusive and forward-looking governance, using technology to preserve heritage and adopting sustainable management practices. In this way, Gulf countries can overcome the challenges of modernisation without compromising the richness of their cultural mosaic. The future is dynamic and holistic, and the identity, unity and resilience of these societies will flourish amid change.

9

Regional Integration
Opportunities and Obstacles

Introduction to Regional Integration: A Strategic Imperative

Efforts towards regional integration in the Gulf have been driven by various factors that emphasise the need for collective cooperation and collaboration. Historical, geopolitical, economic and security considerations have all played an important role in promoting greater regional unity. Rich in natural resources and facing common geopolitical challenges, the Gulf region has long recognised the potential benefits of closer integration. Pursuing economic development and greater stability is one of the main drivers of regional integration. By pooling their resources, leveraging their comparative advantages, and promoting trade liberalisation, Gulf countries aim to establish a robust and resilient economic bloc that can withstand global market fluctuations. Regional integration also enables collective action to address challenges and vulnerabilities, thereby enhancing the overall security of Gulf states. Geopolitical dynamics, characterised by shared concerns about external influences and security threats, further reinforce the need for concerted action and unified strategies among Gulf countries. These motivations are closely linked to the region's history of cooperation, reflecting a recognition of its interdependence and interconnectedness. Thus, the pursuit of greater regional integration is based on the belief that a more coherent and coordinated approach could bring substantial benefits in many areas, ranging from economic diversification and technological progress to diplomatic and geopolitical influence. In summary, the need for economic development, enhanced security and improved geopolitical positioning all emphasise the importance of regional integration in the Gulf, making it a strategic necessity that requires careful consideration and joint action.

Historical perspectives on cooperation in the Gulf

The region's history is rich in diplomatic, economic, and strategic interactions that have shaped its dynamics. From the early days of independence for many Gulf states in the 20th century, leaders recognised the mutual benefits of collaboration in areas such as trade, security and political alignment. The formation of the Arab League in 1945 was a significant milestone, reflecting the initial steps towards unity and coordination among Arab nations, including those in the Gulf. However, the need for strategic cooperation became more acute in the wake of the 1973 oil crisis. The Gulf Cooperation Council (GCC) was established in 1981 to promote unity and integration among the Gulf states. Initially comprising Bahrain, Kuwait, Oman, Qatar, Saudi Arabia and the United Arab Emirates, the GCC has served as a platform for addressing common challenges and seizing opportunities.

Throughout its history, cooperation in the Gulf has been influenced by the evolving geopolitical landscape and global dynamics. Conflicts such as the Iran-Iraq War and the Gulf War have emphasised the importance of collective security measures and diplomatic initiatives. Additionally, economic interdependence linked to the oil industry and diversification efforts has reinforced the importance of regional cooperation. However, historical tensions and rivalries have sometimes hindered sustainable collaboration, with territorial disputes and divergent political agendas occasionally impeding progress. Nevertheless, significant advances have been recorded, including the conclusion of joint defence agreements, the creation of free trade zones, and the adoption of common policies, all of which demonstrate the ongoing evolution of cooperation in the region. Understanding these historical developments is crucial for evaluating the current state and future potential of regional integration in the Gulf.

Institutional frameworks: the GCC and beyond

The Gulf Cooperation Council (GCC) is a symbol of regional unity. It aims to promote collaboration, economic integration, and collective security among its member states. Established in 1981, it comprises six member countries: Bahrain, Kuwait, Oman, Qatar, Saudi Arabia and the United Arab Emirates. The GCC was formed in response to the shared challenges and threats these nations faced, including regional conflicts and security issues. The GCC's institutional framework provides a platform for promoting mutual understanding, cooperation and coordination on various political, economic and social issues. This enables member states to address common challenges and leverage their collective strengths to improve the region. Beyond the GCC, broader efforts towards regional integration extend to neighbouring countries and external partners. These initiatives aim to strengthen economic interdependence, consolidate diplomatic relations, and facilitate the development of cross-border infrastructure. These intergovernmental frameworks and partnerships illustrate the shared vision of an interconnected and prosperous Gulf region. Additionally, the establishment of joint councils, committees, and institutions within the GCC demonstrates a commitment to strengthening ties and harmonising policies, a commitment that is also evident in other regional collaborations. These institutional mechanisms enable member states to engage in dialogue, negotiate agreements, and implement coordinated strategies to address common challenges and capitalise on collective opportunities. As the Gulf region continues to evolve, these institutional frameworks will serve as essential platforms for promoting regional stability, economic prosperity and collaborative problem solving. In the face of emerging global changes and current challenges, the adaptability and effectiveness of these institutional structures are crucial for shaping the future of regional integration and cooperation.

Economic Incentives and Business Opportunities

The Gulf region, with its abundant natural resources and strategic geopolitical location, offers a multitude of economic incentives and business opportunities for regional and international actors. The diversification of economies and reduction of dependence on oil revenues are key priorities for Gulf states, leading to an increased focus on strengthening trade and investment links with global partners. As the global economy continues to grow, the Gulf region is becoming an increasingly attractive market for companies seeking new opportunities and partnerships. The establishment of free trade zones and economic diversification initiatives has further boosted interest in the region. Implementing economic reforms and liberalisation measures has created an environment conducive to foreign direct investment, promoting economic growth and technological progress. Furthermore, the Gulf's commitment to developing infrastructure and innovating, particularly in sectors such as renewable energy, finance, and tourism, has attracted the attention of international investors. The region's strategic location along major trade routes and connectivity with emerging markets make it an ideal hub for transnational trade and investment. By leveraging its comparative advantages and economic potential, the Gulf region is set to become a major player in the global economy. Collaborating with international partners through bilateral and multilateral trade agreements is essential for mutual economic prosperity and growth. Furthermore, participating in regional economic forums and organisations facilitates dialogue and cooperation, paving the way for a more integrated and interconnected global economy. As the Gulf continues to diversify its economy and facilitate trade, it is crucial that policymakers and business leaders actively engage in exploring and exploiting the region's many economic incentives and commercial opportunities.

Political alignments and diplomatic alliances

In the context of regional integration, these alignments play a central role in the Gulf region's dynamics. These are influenced by a complex network of historical, economic, and security factors, often leading to strategic partnerships between Gulf states and other global actors. These alignments are shaped by shared interests, values, and geopolitical objectives. Diplomatic alliances, on the other hand, involve formal agreements and treaties aimed at strengthening cooperation and addressing common challenges. Such alliances are vital for fostering mutual understanding and trust between nations. When examining the landscape of political alignments, it is important to consider the range of actors involved, including major powers, neighbouring states and international organisations. The interaction between these actors and their respective agendas can significantly impact the region's stability and development. Historically, Gulf states have engaged in various forms of alignment, ranging from bilateral partnerships to multilateral coalitions, reflecting diverse interests and priorities. Furthermore, the evolving geopolitical landscape has led to the redefinition of traditional alliances and the emergence of novel cooperation frameworks. To understand these alignments, it is necessary to examine historical contexts, power dynamics and shifting alliances in response to regional and global developments. In addition to political alignments, this chapter explores diplomatic alliances, emphasising how formalised relations can promote peace, security and prosperity. By forming diplomatic alliances, Gulf states can strengthen their collective influence on the international stage while preserving their sovereignty and national interests. These alliances also serve as essential mechanisms for resolving conflicts, easing tensions and advancing common goals such as economic development, regional security and cultural exchange. Through an in-depth analysis of political alignments and diplomatic alliances, we will provide an overview of the complex network of interstate relations that underpins the dynamics of regional integration in the Gulf. Examining the historical evolution and contemporary manifestations of these alignments helps readers to understand the opportunities and challenges of promoting cohesive and collaborative ties among Gulf states and with external actors.

Cultural and social cohesion initiatives

Cultural and social cohesion initiatives play a vital role in promoting unity and solidarity among Gulf nations. Drawing on the region's rich diversity of traditions and customs, these initiatives aim to strengthen social cohesion and foster a collective identity.

One of the main areas of focus is the preservation and promotion of cultural heritage, with an emphasis on traditional arts, crafts, music, and literature that reflect the unique mosaic of Gulf societies. This instils a sense of pride and belonging in the population, thereby reinforcing the shared historical narratives that unite these nations. Additionally, initiatives that promote dialogue and intercultural understanding help to bridge social divides, fostering mutual respect and empathy. By facilitating platforms for dialogue and open exchange, Gulf states can promote inclusion and a mutual appreciation of their cultural heritage's richness. Efforts to promote social cohesion also address societal challenges and encourage community engagement. Programmes focused on social welfare, education, and healthcare improve people's living conditions and strengthen social stability and cohesion. Furthermore, encouraging volunteerism and civic participation enables individuals to contribute actively to the improvement of their communities, thereby strengthening social ties. Embracing the values of tolerance and acceptance enables Gulf countries to promote social cohesion initiatives that celebrate diversity and foster a sense of belonging for all members of society. Through concerted efforts to promote cultural exchanges, preserve heritage, and address social needs, Gulf countries can forge stronger ties and lay the foundations for a more integrated and harmonious regional community.

Security cooperation: counterterrorism and defence

The security landscape in the Gulf region is closely linked to the global fight against terrorism and the need to protect national borders from external threats. In recognition of the transnational nature of security challenges, Gulf countries are strengthening their collaboration to combat terrorism and defend their territory. This is particularly relevant given the growing presence of non-state actors and the potential spillover effects of conflicts in neighbouring regions. Security efforts are being integrated through intelligence sharing, joint military exercises and coordinated border control initiatives. These initiatives demonstrate a commitment to collective security and constitute a proactive measure to prevent any force that could destabilise the region. Furthermore, by harmonising their defence strategies, Gulf countries are enhancing their ability to respond swiftly and effectively to emerging security threats, thereby setting a precedent for regional cooperation. These collaborations are based on the principles of mutual assistance and solidarity, thereby reinforcing the region's security architecture. However, it is important to recognise that, while security collaborations have clear advantages, they also present inherent complexities. Each nation retains its sovereignty and specific security interests, which can sometimes lead to differences in priorities and approaches. Furthermore, historical rivalries and differing perceptions of threats among Gulf states can hinder smooth security integration. Nevertheless, Gulf countries are overcoming these obstacles through open dialogue and negotiation to forge strong partnerships aimed at ensuring greater stability in the region. Case studies illustrating successful joint operations and unified responses to security crises provide valuable insights into the practical benefits of collaboration in counterterrorism and defence. The lessons learned from these initiatives inform future strategies and emphasise the vital importance of sustained multilateral engagement in strengthening the Gulf region's security architecture. Looking to the future, evolving security collaborations will remain central to the region's capacity to address both traditional and emerging threats, thereby contributing to a more secure and stable Gulf region.

Obstacles to integration include political rivalries and a lack of trust

Regional integration in the Gulf is hindered by numerous obstacles related to deep-rooted political rivalries and distrust between member states. The historical context of competition and power struggles has led to deep-seated scepticism and mistrust, hindering the progress of collaborative initiatives. Political rivalries, often linked to divergent strategic interests and ideological differences, hinder the ability to reach agreement on key issues and reduce the potential for effective cooperation. Additionally, historical conflicts and disputes have perpetuated a climate of mistrust, making it challenging to forge robust and enduring partnerships. A lack of shared vision for regional integration exacerbates these obstacles further, as different priorities and aspirations hinder coordinated efforts. Political rivalries manifest in various ways, including different foreign policy orientations, conflicting national agendas, and competing alliances with external powers. These dynamics generate tensions that overshadow the potential benefits of integration, perpetuating a climate of uncertainty and insecurity. The resulting trust deficit further complicates integration efforts, as historical grievances and perceived betrayals continue to shape interstate relations. This lack of mutual trust undermines the foundations necessary for effective collaboration and jeopardises the success of regional integration. Furthermore, the absence of transparent dispute resolution and communication mechanisms exacerbates the trust deficit, perpetuating a cycle of alienation and suspicion. Bridging the gap between political rivals and restoring trust is a daunting task, but an essential one for further regional integration. Overcoming these obstacles requires sustained dialogue, confidence-building measures and a commitment to fostering mutual understanding and respect. Any initiatives addressing political rivalries and the trust deficit must be underpinned by confidence-building efforts and transparent communication channels. It will also be essential to foster a sense of shared purpose through comprehensive, inclusive strategies that address these challenges. By addressing the root causes of political rivalries and the trust deficit, the Gulf region can pave the way for enhanced cooperation, greater resilience, and collective prosperity.

Case studies: success stories and lessons learned

To analyse the landscape of regional integration in the Gulf, it is imperative to study case studies that illustrate successful initiatives and lessons learned from failures. The United Arab Emirates is a prime example of successful regional integration, thanks to its forward-looking strategy focusing on economic diversification, technological innovation, and investment in education. Its vision of becoming a knowledge-based economy has fostered collaboration between sectors, giving rise to strong partnerships and synergies within the country and with neighbouring nations. This case study serves as an inspiration for realising regional potential and emphasises the importance of long-term planning and visionary leadership.

In contrast, the diplomatic rift within the Gulf Cooperation Council (GCC) has revealed the complexities and challenges involved in maintaining regional integration. The blockade imposed on Qatar by several GCC member states exposed tensions within the region. This case study provides valuable insights into the delicate balance of power, and demonstrates the impact that divergent geopolitical interests can have on regional cohesion. It emphasises the importance of principled dialogue, conflict resolution mechanisms, and sustained efforts to transcend political rivalries.

Furthermore, the success of King Abdullah Economic City in Saudi Arabia demonstrates the transformative potential of cross-border economic zones in fostering regional synergies. Through strategic investment and infrastructure development, this initiative has strengthened cross-border trade links and collaboration, thereby contributing to the broader goal of consolidating regional economic integration. In contrast, the abandonment of the monetary union project among the GCC states highlights the importance of consensus building and shared governance structures, as well as the need to adopt a gradual approach to monetary integration.

Oman's proactive engagement in regional mediation and peacebuilding efforts highlights the vital role of diplomatic influence in strengthening regional ties and fostering trust. By facilitating dialogue and providing a neutral venue for diplomatic discussions, Oman demonstrates the importance of constructive engagement and outreach activities in fostering regional cooperation.

These case studies highlight the multifaceted nature of successes and setbacks in regional integration, emphasising the importance of visionary leadership, political will, inclusivity and conflict resolution mechanisms. These examples of triumphs and trials provide essential lessons for charting the path towards enhanced regional unity in the Gulf.

Looking ahead: towards enhanced regional unity

The future of regional integration in the Gulf presents a mix of challenges and opportunities for stakeholders operating in a complex geopolitical landscape. Clearly, the path towards enhanced regional unity is multifaceted and requires strategic, collective efforts from all concerned parties. It is important to explore avenues and strategies that could foster greater unity among Gulf countries.

A crucial aspect that deserves particular attention is the need for inclusive dialogue and sustained engagement to address divergent interests and foster mutual understanding. Recognising common goals while accepting diversity can lay the foundation for trust and cooperation. Proactively harmonising policies on economic integration, security partnerships, and cultural exchanges is also essential for a holistic approach to unity. Exploring mechanisms to strengthen economic interdependence and reduce trade barriers, for example, could enhance regional stability and prosperity. Furthermore, initiatives to strengthen security cooperation and intelligence sharing can help form a united front against common threats, thereby strengthening mutual trust. Cultural and educational exchanges play a vital role in raising awareness and promoting goodwill between cultures, thereby helping to forge a strong regional identity. Celebrating shared heritage while understanding and respecting differences can strengthen social cohesion and create lasting bonds between diverse communities. Overcoming obstacles to unity, such as historical rivalries and political tensions, will require bold diplomatic efforts, patience, and compromise. Learning from successful examples and valuable lessons from past initiatives can inform future approaches to regional integration. Using technology and innovation to bridge gaps and promote digital connectivity can pave the way for enhanced regional unity. Adopting sustainable development practices and responsible environmental management can contribute to regional unity by transcending national borders for the collective benefit. Investing in people-to-people interactions and local initiatives can foster positive change from the ground up, strengthening a sense of shared destiny and responsibility. Finally, strengthening the capacity and effectiveness of regional institutions and frameworks is essential to steer the process towards greater regional unity. By valuing their shared principles, goals and resources, the Gulf countries can forge a new path towards a more integrated, resilient and prosperous regional community.

10
Scenarios for the Future
Risks and Resilience

Scenario planning

Scenario planning is a strategic tool that gives organisations and decision-makers a structured way of anticipating and managing future uncertainties. In an increasingly complex and interconnected world, the ability to navigate uncertainty and ambiguity is essential for long-term success. By systematically exploring a range of plausible future scenarios, organisations can prepare for a variety of potential outcomes and make more informed decisions. This proactive approach enables them to identify early warning signs, adapt to changing circumstances, and capitalise on emerging opportunities.

The importance of scenario planning lies in its ability to challenge assumptions and promote a holistic view of the future. Rather than making predictions or forecasts based on linear extrapolations, it encourages stakeholders to consider the multiple dimensions and nonlinear trends that could influence future developments. This enables organisations to break free from the constraints of current assumptions and consider alternative futures, thereby strengthening their strategic resilience.

Fundamentally, scenario planning acknowledges the unpredictability of the future while providing a structured framework for considering a range of possibilities. This methodology helps to identify the driving forces and critical uncertainties that could affect the organisation's environment, enabling a more thorough risk assessment and strategic preparedness. By accepting uncertainty as a given and actively addressing it, organisations can foster a culture of strategic foresight and adaptability.

Furthermore, scenario planning is a valuable decision-making tool in highly complex and ambiguous contexts. It fosters a flexible and prepared mindset, enabling organisations to respond swiftly to unexpected events and disruptions. Furthermore, by systematically analysing different scenarios, decision-makers can identify robust strategies capable of withstanding a wide range of potential future situations.

As we explore the nuances of scenario planning further, it becomes evident that this strategic practice transcends mere forecasting. It embodies a proactive approach to the future, empowering organisations to proactively shape their destiny. Through scenario planning, organisations can mitigate risks, seize opportunities, and cultivate the forward-looking orientation that is essential for thriving in an uncertain world.

Methodology and analytical frameworks

Developing robust scenarios for the future of the Gulf requires a comprehensive and rigorous methodology supported by various analytical frameworks. This approach is based on the understanding that the region's geopolitical, economic, and social dynamics are complex and require a multifaceted analytical approach. First, historical data and trends are examined in detail to establish a baseline for forecasting future trajectories. This involves an in-depth study of demographic changes, technological advances, energy consumption patterns, and regional political developments. Using quantitative and qualitative methods such as statistical analysis, trend extrapolation and expert consultations further enhances the analysis's credibility and depth. Meanwhile, various analytical frameworks — including scenario-building tools such as the 2x2 matrix and layered causal analysis — allow contrasting futures to be explored, identifying the main factors shaping these divergent paths. Furthermore, integrating risk assessment models, decision trees and Monte Carlo simulations enables the assessment of probabilistic outcomes and potential unforeseeable events. The framework also recognises critical uncertainties and their potential impact on the future of the Gulf. This requires unpredictable variables and alternative futures to be integrated into the analysis. Stakeholder engagement and participatory workshops are integral to the methodology, ensuring that the diverse perspectives of experts in the field are considered in scenario development. Considering global megatrends such as climate change, technological disruption and shifting power dynamics provides a global context for considering the future of the Gulf. It is important to recognise that the methodology acknowledges the nonlinear nature of change and the interaction between various systems, necessitating a dynamic and adaptable analytical approach. Consequently, dynamic modelling and system dynamics techniques are employed to provide a holistic view of complex interactions and feedback loops. Overall, the scenario planning methodology adopted in this context is inherently interdisciplinary, incorporating elements of geopolitics, economics, sociology, environmental studies, and strategic foresight. Weaving these different threads together provides a solid basis for developing compelling and insightful scenarios that highlight the risks and resilience of the Gulf's future.

Reference trends: current trajectories

In order to understand the potential future trajectories of the Gulf region, it is crucial to first grasp the reference trends that are currently shaping its landscape. Our aim is to delve deeper into the interdependent economic, political and social factors that currently define the region's course.

Economically, most Gulf states continue to depend on hydrocarbons as their main source of revenue, despite concerted efforts towards diversification. This dependence has shaped the region's economic trajectory and made it vulnerable to fluctuations in the global energy market. Furthermore, dominant demographic trends, such as rapid population growth and large youth populations, influence consumption patterns, labour markets and social dynamics, impacting the direction of development. In geopolitical terms, historical alliances, security agreements and regional rivalries continue to play a central role in the Gulf region's evolution. The socio-political landscape is characterised by evolving national identities, social movements, and shifts in governance structures, all of which contribute to the region's ongoing transformation. Additionally, the environmental context is crucial, as the implications of climate change, water scarcity, and ecological degradation pose significant challenges to sustainable development in the region. Mapping these underlying trends provides a comprehensive understanding of the factors shaping the Gulf's current trajectories, setting the stage for further exploration of potential disruptors and alternative future scenarios.

Potential disruptors are variables that could significantly alter the status quo

The Gulf region is at a critical juncture, facing potential disruptors that could alter its current trajectory. Several game-changing variables have emerged, posing complex challenges to traditional analytical and policy frameworks. Geopolitical dynamics, technological advances, and socio-economic changes are among the key disruptive factors requiring in-depth analysis. On the geopolitical front, for example, evolving relations between regional and global powers could introduce unprecedented uncertainties affecting trade, security alliances, and diplomatic norms. Technological upheavals, particularly in the energy sector — including advances in renewable energies and transformative digital innovations — are likely to reshape the energy landscape and economic structures. Furthermore, socio-economic changes driven by demographic shifts, the aspirations of young people and social movements could lead to new patterns of demand, new employment dynamics and new expectations regarding governance. Climate change and environmental degradation are also disruptive forces impacting resource availability, infrastructure resilience and human security. In order to arrive at a more comprehensive understanding of future scenarios for the Gulf, it is necessary to analyse these key disruptive factors in depth, taking into account their interdependence and potential synergies. In order to anticipate and effectively manage these potential disruptive factors, a forward-looking approach is necessary, drawing on strategic vision and scenario planning to proactively address future challenges and capitalise on emerging opportunities. By closely examining these game-changing variables, policymakers can better prepare for the complexities of the future, ensuring resilience and adaptability in a rapidly changing geopolitical landscape.

Scenario 1: Continuity amid change

As we explore the complex future of the Gulf region, Scenario 1 offers a compelling vision of how countries could maintain stability and progress amid change. The basic assumption in this scenario is that although external forces and internal challenges may cause significant change, the fundamental structures and relationships within Gulf states will remain resilient and adaptable. This continuity is underpinned by proactive leadership, robust institutions, and strategic foresight. Economically, sustained diversification efforts and investment in non-oil sectors provide a solid foundation for growth and mitigate the impact of volatility in global energy markets. Technological advances and innovation also drive productivity gains, thereby strengthening competitive advantages in key industries. Geopolitically, proactive diplomacy and cooperative regional initiatives enable Gulf countries to address external pressures and conflicts collectively, thereby promoting mutual stability and security. Socio-politically, inclusive governance models and social reforms ensure demographic changes and the population's aspirations are considered, thereby promoting social cohesion and harmony. Furthermore, proactive measures to address environmental concerns and promote sustainable development further emphasise this commitment to continuity in a changing environment. While this scenario embodies resilience and adaptability, it also recognises the need to maintain a proactive approach and prepare for unexpected challenges.

Scenario 2: Navigating Instability

In the face of geopolitical, economic, and social turbulence, this scenario highlights the ability to successfully navigate instability within the Gulf region. This scenario is based on factors such as sudden changes in global energy markets, intensifying regional tensions, and internal socio-economic pressures. In a context of growing uncertainty, governments, businesses and communities must grapple with the complexity of maintaining stability in a constantly changing environment. At the heart of this scenario lies the delicate balance between security, strategic decision-making, and promoting resilience.

The potential disruptions inherent in this scenario require a deep understanding of the multifaceted risks facing Gulf states. From heightened security threats to economic vulnerabilities, stakeholders must closely monitor developments in order to anticipate and respond to potential crises. This proactive approach necessitates robust contingency plans, effective risk management frameworks and adaptive governance structures.

Furthermore, to navigate instability, the interaction between internal reforms and external commitments must be assessed with nuance. The ability to adapt policies dynamically, demonstrate institutional flexibility, and maintain social cohesion is crucial for responding to destabilising forces. Scenario 2 also implies reassessing traditional alliances, strategic partnerships, and diplomatic approaches, as well as exploring innovative solutions for conflict resolution and collaborative crisis management.

In the face of these challenges, innovation and agility are paramount. Scenario 2 emphasises the importance of embracing technological advances, leveraging human capital, and adopting sustainable development practices to promote stability in times of turmoil. Promoting a culture of adaptability, creativity and foresight is also essential to prepare for sudden disruptions and mitigate their effects.

In conclusion, Scenario 2 highlights the need to strengthen adaptive capacity, proactive governance, and strategic foresight in order to navigate the instability in the Gulf region. Addressing the multiple dimensions of risk, mobilising collective efforts towards resilience, and harnessing the transformative potential of innovation will enable us to navigate uncertain waters and emerge stronger from instability.

Scenario 3: Wave of innovation and reform

In Scenario 3, we envisage a future for the Gulf region characterised by a wave of innovation and reform. This scenario explores the potential for transformative change, driven by technological advances, visionary leadership, and societal demand for progress. Amidst the region's complex dynamics, this scenario offers an optimistic outlook based on proactive adaptations and forward-looking strategies. This wave of innovation and reform encompasses economic diversification, governance reform, social development, and environmental sustainability. Above all, it symbolises the Gulf countries' ability to embrace change and lead the way in charting a new course. Economic diversification is central to this scenario, with Gulf countries leveraging their resources and expertise to develop a diversified and resilient economy. A focus on emerging industries, renewable energy and knowledge-based sectors is becoming the hallmark of this transformative vision, moving the region away from its overreliance on hydrocarbons. Governance reform is also key to this wave of innovation and reform. Forward-thinking leaders are undertaking comprehensive institutional restructuring and establishing accountability mechanisms and inclusive decision-making processes to promote transparency and efficiency. Social development is shifting towards inclusive growth, with investment in human capital and the empowerment of marginalised communities to promote social cohesion and prosperity. Environmental sustainability is also becoming a top priority, with concerted efforts towards green initiatives, conservation, and climate resilience positioning the Gulf as a global leader in sustainable development. This wave of innovation and reform is also catalysing cross-sector collaboration, knowledge exchange, and strategic partnerships, thereby amplifying the region's influence and impact on the global stage. By embarking on this transformative path, the Gulf is emerging as a beacon of progressive change, inspiring others and shaping new paradigms on the international stage. Nevertheless, this scenario is not without challenges, requiring resolute commitment, adaptability and skilful management of complexities. Nevertheless, it offers a compelling vision of resilience and evolution, driven by a collective determination to shape a prosperous and inclusive future for the Gulf and its people.

Resilience strategies: strengthening adaptive capacities

As we explore the complex landscape of future scenarios facing the Gulf region, it is becoming increasingly clear that the need for such strategies and capacities is paramount. Building resilience involves proactively preparing and strengthening social, economic, and political systems to withstand and recover from disruptive events. In the Gulf context, this requires a multifaceted approach integrating innovative governance, diversified economic frameworks, and social cohesion. A fundamental pillar of resilience is strengthening adaptive capacity, referring to the ability of systems and societies to adjust to changing conditions. This capacity can be cultivated through various strategic measures, including investing in human capital, diversifying key sectors, and implementing institutional reforms.

Recognising the interdependence of risks and opportunities in the Gulf region is imperative to effectively strengthening this capacity. This requires the establishment of robust risk assessment and management mechanisms, the promotion of cross-sectoral collaboration and the strengthening of information-sharing platforms. Furthermore, fostering a culture of innovation and embracing technological advances can significantly bolster the adaptive capacity of Gulf states.

Harnessing the potential of digital transformation, renewable energy solutions, and sustainable resource management enables the region to proactively adapt to evolving challenges and seize emerging opportunities. Resilience strategies must also be based on a thorough understanding of the social, environmental, and geopolitical dynamics that will shape the future of the Gulf region.

This requires engagement with various stakeholders, such as academia, the private sector and civil society organisations, to encourage inclusive dialogue and holistic problem-solving approaches. Promoting a culture of proactive risk communication and encouraging public participation is also essential to strengthen societal resilience.

Strategic investments in physical and social infrastructure are vital for strengthening the adaptive capacity of Gulf countries. Whether through resilient urban planning or strengthening health and education systems, these initiatives can significantly enhance the region's capacity to withstand shocks and transition towards sustainable development pathways. Effective regulatory frameworks and policy coherence also play a critical role in promoting adaptive capacity by ensuring that decisions align with long-term resilience objectives.

It is important to emphasise that efforts to strengthen adaptive capacity and resilience are ongoing processes that require continuous monitoring, evaluation and adaptation. A forward-looking vision that anticipates and prepares for potential disruptive forces is vital for promoting resilience across the Gulf region. In the next section, we will conduct a comparative analysis of resilience efforts in other global contexts to identify valuable lessons and best practices that can inform the development of resilience strategies in the Gulf.

Comparative analysis: lessons from global peers

As the Gulf region navigates an increasingly complex geopolitical landscape, examining the experiences of global peers facing similar challenges and opportunities can provide valuable insights. Examining the experiences of regions such as East Asia, Europe and North America can inform strategic decision-making and policy development. In East Asia, for instance, countries have experienced territorial disputes, energy security concerns and economic interdependence — dynamics that mirror some of the trends observed in the Gulf. Studying how these nations have established cooperation agreements, managed their rivalries and diversified their economies could provide valuable lessons for Gulf leaders. Similarly, Europe's experience with regional integration and managing diverse national interests can offer useful insights into the complexities of consensus-building and cooperation within the Gulf Cooperation Council (GCC) and beyond. Furthermore, North America's experience of using technological innovation to address environmental challenges and promote sustainable development could inspire the Gulf to develop initiatives to combat climate change and transition to a more diversified and resilient economy. This comparative analysis enables Gulf stakeholders to draw on a wealth of global experience, adapt effective strategies and avoid pitfalls by building on results observed elsewhere. Adopting a forward-looking approach that integrates global lessons into local contexts will strengthen the Gulf region's position in addressing future uncertainties and capitalising on new opportunities.

In conclusion

Comparing the Gulf region with other regions of the world provides valuable insights for developing future strategies. It is clear that the challenges facing the Gulf are linked to broader global dynamics when lessons are drawn from diverse contexts. Furthermore, the successes and failures of other regions offer a rich mosaic of experiences from which to learn best practices and identify potential pitfalls. This comparative analysis underscores the need for an adaptive, forward-looking approach. It emphasises the importance of leveraging global knowledge networks and engaging in interregional dialogue to foster innovation and resilience.

Synthesising scenarios for the future of the Gulf region reveals the multifaceted nature of risks and opportunities. Each scenario provides a distinct viewpoint on various potential future trajectories, offering a thorough exploration of possible futures. From pursuing continuity amid change, to managing instability, to riding the wave of innovation and reform, these narratives provide a rich palette for navigating the uncertainties ahead. The aim of this exercise is not to predict the future with extreme precision, but rather to develop robust strategies that can withstand the dynamic forces shaping the Gulf region.

As we delve deeper into the strategic implications drawn from the synthesised scenarios, it becomes clear that flexibility and agility are paramount. In a context of fluid global dynamics, an adaptive mindset is required that transcends rigid doctrines and favours the development of iterative strategies. Furthermore, fostering collaboration and synergies across sectors and stakeholders appears to be essential for strengthening resilience. This involves forming new alliances, leveraging technological advances and investing in human capital in order to proactively address challenges and seize emerging opportunities.

The strategic implications also highlight the central role of governance and policy frameworks in determining the way forward. Balancing the imperatives of security, economic diversification, and environmental sustainability requires nuanced policy responses that prioritise long-term resilience over short-term gains. This necessitates adjusting regulatory frameworks and institutional structures to align with the evolving needs of Gulf societies and the global community.

In conclusion, synthesising the divergent perspectives explored in this chapter emphasises the necessity of a holistic, forward-looking approach to managing risk and resilience in the Gulf region. By fostering a culture of continuous learning, informed decision-making, and proactive adaptation, Gulf countries can weather potential storms and thrive in an uncertain context. The strategic implications derived from this narrative will guide policymakers, academics and practitioners as they work together to steer the Gulf region towards a future characterised by sustainable progress and resilience.

11
Policy Implications
Strategic Choices for Gulf Leaders

Strategic assessment: evaluation of current policies

This involves an in-depth review of existing policy frameworks to identify their respective strengths, weaknesses, opportunities and threats. In the context of Gulf leadership, this process involves carefully examining economic strategies, security policies, diplomatic initiatives, and social development programmes.

Analysing current policies enables leaders to identify areas requiring adjustment in order to adapt to changing regional and global dynamics. The assessment considers not only financial and military factors, but also various facets of governance, such as cultural preservation, environmental sustainability and technological progress.

A key aspect of this assessment is analysing the effectiveness of current policies in promoting regional stability, prosperity and resilience. Leaders must also evaluate the impact of their decisions on societal well-being, inclusive growth and international relations. They must also assess how adaptable policies are in the face of unforeseen challenges such as geopolitical changes, economic disruptions and environmental crises. Through this process, Gulf leaders can gain valuable insights into the effectiveness of their governance approaches and pinpoint areas in need of strategic reorientation.

Strategic assessment also requires a nuanced analysis of the alignment between current policies and long-term national objectives. This involves examining the extent to which existing strategies contribute to achieving overall development goals such as economic diversification, social empowerment, and environmental preservation. It also involves exploring potential synergies and conflicts between different policy areas to ensure a holistic and coherent approach to governance. This scrutiny provides the basis for informed decision-making and sound policy adjustments, enabling the realisation of the desired future for the Gulf region.

Additionally, a thorough strategic assessment takes a forward-looking perspective to examine the anticipatory capacity of current policies. Leaders in the Gulf region must evaluate the flexibility and anticipatory capacity of their current frameworks in order to proactively address future challenges and opportunities. This involves anticipating how emerging technologies, demographic changes and global trends will affect the effectiveness and relevance of policies. By conducting such rigorous analysis, leaders can position themselves at the forefront of governance, preparing themselves to navigate uncertainty while leveraging transformative trends for their respective nations and the region as a whole.

Regional cooperation: leveraging collective strengths

Regional cooperation is an essential means for Gulf leaders to leverage their collective strengths to address common challenges and seize shared opportunities. The interdependence and shared interests of Gulf countries highlight the potential advantages of closer collaboration in areas such as trade, security, and development.

Strategically aligning their policies and initiatives can help Gulf leaders create a more resilient and united region, thereby strengthening its stability and prosperity. At the heart of regional cooperation lies the urgent need to build strategic alliances that transcend individual national interests.

Through diplomatic dialogue and multilateral agreements, Gulf leaders can strengthen their capacity to address common threats, such as terrorism, maritime security and geopolitical pressures. Information sharing, joint military exercises and intelligence collaboration can reinforce the collective security architecture, thereby building confidence and deterrence against external disruptions.

Economic integration also plays a crucial role in regional cooperation. Creating common markets, facilitating cross-border investment, and harmonising regulatory frameworks can amplify the region's economic potential and resilience. Leveraging their comparative advantages and promoting intra-regional trade enables Gulf countries to mitigate the impact of global market fluctuations and diversify their economies, reducing their dependence on hydrocarbons. Additionally, pooling resources and developing infrastructure projects can stimulate innovation, connectivity, and sustainable growth throughout the region.

Furthermore, cultural and social exchanges are an essential element of regional cooperation, fostering understanding and solidarity among diverse populations. Educational collaborations, tourism initiatives and artistic projects can cultivate a sense of shared identity and mutual respect, transcending borders and enriching the social fabric. This convergence of cultures strengthens social cohesion and serves as a bridge for interaction between peoples, paving the way for deeper cooperation in various fields.

Coordinated regional action is also required to address environmental challenges that transcend national borders. By collectively investing in renewable energy projects, conservation measures and climate adaptation strategies, Gulf countries can honour their commitment to sustainability and environmental resilience. This concerted approach to environmental protection preserves natural ecosystems and strengthens the Gulf's global position as a responsible steward of the environment.

In short, regional cooperation is a strategic necessity for Gulf leaders as it enables them to overcome collective challenges and capitalise on shared opportunities. Adopting a mindset of unity and collaboration will enable Gulf countries to strengthen their resilience, stimulate growth, and foster a harmonious regional ecosystem that can thrive in a changing global context.

Economic reforms: diversification and sustainability

The Gulf region has always been heavily dependent on revenues from the hydrocarbon industry. However, given the changing global energy landscape and the urgent need to address environmental issues, economic diversification and sustainability have become paramount. This transition requires a strategic adjustment of economic policies to reduce dependence on oil and gas, and to promote new avenues for growth and development. This may involve investing in non-oil sectors such as tourism, technology, finance and renewable energy. Sustainability involves adopting responsible resource management practices, promoting green initiatives, and seeking clean energy solutions. Such reforms would mitigate the risk of economic vulnerability linked to oil price fluctuations and pave the way for a more balanced, resilient and environmentally friendly economy. Furthermore, diversification and sustainability initiatives can create opportunities for job creation, talent retention, and the expansion of a knowledge-based economy, establishing the Gulf as a hub for innovation and entrepreneurship. To achieve this, governments and policymakers must collaborate closely with industry stakeholders, academia and international partners to develop comprehensive strategies that promote economic diversification and sustainability. At the same time, it is essential that these reforms are inclusive and benefit all segments of society, thereby strengthening social cohesion and stability. Ultimately, these economic reforms focused on diversification and sustainability are a proactive response to the changing global economic landscape, serving as catalysts for long-term prosperity and resilience in the Gulf region.

Security frameworks: balancing defence and diplomacy

In the complex geopolitical landscape of the Gulf, striking a balance between defence and diplomacy is crucial for ensuring regional stability and security. Security frameworks in this context involve not only military capabilities, but also strategic diplomatic initiatives aimed at encouraging peaceful coexistence and mitigating potential conflicts. Achieving this balance requires a multidimensional approach that considers both conventional and unconventional threats while engaging in dialogue and negotiation with regional and international actors. One aspect of this balance is the judicious allocation of resources to defence capabilities, while emphasising the importance of diplomatic channels for conflict resolution and crisis management. In the face of growing asymmetric threats, such as cyber warfare, terrorism, and non-state actors, a comprehensive security framework must be adaptable and forward-looking. It must incorporate technological advances and intelligence sharing in order to stay ahead of new challenges. Furthermore, a balanced approach involves cultivating strong alliances and partnerships with like-minded nations and actively participating in regional security forums and cooperation agreements to address common threats collectively. Proactive diplomatic engagement should not be viewed as a sign of weakness, but rather as a pragmatic and effective means of easing tensions and fostering trust between neighbouring countries. At the same time, maintaining a credible deterrence posture is crucial to demonstrate resolve and deter potential aggressors. Effective security frameworks require an in-depth understanding of the evolving nature of conflicts, integrating non-military instruments of national power — such as economic levers and soft power — to influence adversarial behaviour and promote stability. Continuous assessment of geopolitical dynamics and recalibration of defence and diplomatic strategies based on these assessments are essential to ensure agility and responsiveness. Ultimately, achieving a balance between defence and diplomacy in the Gulf region requires wise leadership, a long-term vision, and a commitment to maintaining peace and security for the collective well-being of all stakeholders.

Innovation and technology policies are drivers of future growth

In today's interconnected world, the rapid pace of technological progress presents the Gulf region with unprecedented opportunities and challenges. As Gulf leaders navigate the complexities of a rapidly changing global landscape, recognising the central role of innovation and technology in future growth and prosperity is imperative. Let's examine the strategic policies and initiatives needed to harness the transformative power of innovation and technology.

To foster an environment conducive to innovation, Gulf leaders must prioritise investment in research and development, encourage creativity and risk-taking, and promote a robust ecosystem for entrepreneurship and start-ups. By empowering the brightest minds and encouraging cross-sector collaboration, the Gulf region can establish itself as a leader in technological innovation, paving the way for sustainable economic diversification and global competitiveness.

Developing comprehensive technology policies focused on digital transformation, artificial intelligence, and advanced manufacturing will also be essential for accelerating the region's transition to a knowledge-based economy. Adopting advanced technologies can optimise production processes and improve operational efficiency across all sectors, thereby strengthening the Gulf's position as a hub for innovation-driven economic growth.

Integrating smart infrastructure and sustainable urban planning with innovative technologies will lay the foundations for tomorrow's smart cities in the Gulf. Leveraging advances in connectivity, data analytics, and cybersecurity will enhance residents' quality of life, boost economic productivity, and foster a business- and investment-friendly environment.

It is also crucial to prioritise upgrading and reskilling the workforce to meet the demands of an increasingly digital economy. Strategic partnerships with leading educational institutions and collaborative initiatives with international technology giants can provide the necessary expertise and knowledge transfer to build a highly skilled and adaptable workforce capable of thriving in the Fourth Industrial Revolution.

As the Gulf opens up to technological disruption, robust regulatory frameworks and policies are essential for managing the ethical, legal, and security implications of emerging technologies. Taking proactive measures to protect data privacy, intellectual property rights and cybersecurity will build trust and attract foreign investment, as well as stimulating domestic innovation.

Ultimately, by adopting a bold approach to innovation and technology policy, Gulf leaders can foster an environment where creativity, ingenuity, and technological excellence converge to propel the region into a new era of sustainable economic growth, global influence, and prosperity.

Cultural and social planning: embracing change

In the Gulf's evolving landscape, the importance of long-term cultural and social planning is paramount. As the region embarks on economic diversification and technological advancement, it is crucial to ensure that traditional values and social structures evolve in harmony. Embracing change requires a nuanced approach that recognises the rich diversity of Gulf societies while promoting progressive attitudes towards gender equality, diversity, and inclusion.

Thorough analysis of education systems, media representation and public discourse is required for cultural and social planning. By rethinking educational programmes to foster critical thinking, creativity, and global awareness, Gulf leaders can nurture a generation that can thrive in an ever-changing world. Similarly, promoting diverse and authentic narratives across various media can dispel stereotypes and encourage social inclusion.

Furthermore, embracing change necessitates re-evaluating governance structures and legal frameworks to guarantee human rights, social justice and ethical practices. Empowering marginalised communities, amplifying their voices, and implementing policies that protect their rights are essential to fostering a cohesive and resilient society. Additionally, initiatives to preserve cultural heritage and support the arts strengthen national identity and help revitalise the cultural landscape.

Accepting change also extends to the business world, where organisations are increasingly recognising the value of diversity and adopting inclusive practices. By prioritising ethical business conduct and offering opportunities for professional advancement regardless of gender, nationality, or origin, companies can harness the full potential of a diverse workforce and contribute to social progress.

In summary, long-term cultural and social planning requires a holistic approach to guide the Gulf towards a future characterised by unity in diversity, respect for traditions, innovation, social cohesion and individual empowerment. This requires concerted efforts from leaders, institutions, and citizens alike to uphold progressive values while preserving the region's rich heritage. Embracing change is not only a necessity; it is also an opportunity to propel the Gulf towards a prosperous, inclusive, and sustainable future.

Energy and environmental policy: leading the transition

With the Gulf region at the crossroads of the global energy transition, the need for sustainable energy and environmental policies has never been more urgent. Recognising the interdependence of energy security, economic prosperity and environmental stewardship, Gulf leaders are committed to charting a course that aligns with international efforts to mitigate climate change and adapt to the evolving energy landscape. To this end, the integration of renewable energy, energy efficiency measures and carbon emission reductions is essential. Promoting the development and adoption of renewable energy technologies, such as solar and wind power, will enable us to diversify our energy sources and reduce our dependence on traditional hydrocarbons. Furthermore, investing in research and infrastructure for energy storage and smart grid technologies will stabilise and enhance the reliability of renewable energy systems, thereby accelerating the transition to a low-carbon future. At the same time, strict environmental regulations and environmentally friendly practices must be implemented across all sectors to minimise ecological impact and promote sustainable development. As Gulf countries continue to diversify their economies, adopting clean technologies and sustainable practices demonstrates their commitment to environmental preservation, promoting innovation and competitiveness on the global stage. Additionally, diplomatic engagement and collaboration with international organisations and neighbouring states are vital for harmonising energy and environmental policies, ensuring regional coherence and effectiveness. By forging partnerships for technology transfer, knowledge sharing, and coordinated climate action, Gulf leaders can amplify their influence in shaping global environmental agendas while preserving their own ecological heritage. Public awareness and education initiatives on environmental conservation and sustainable lifestyles further reinforce the overall strategy of leading the transition to a green economy and resilient ecosystems. Encouraging renewable energy projects, promoting green entrepreneurship and integrating environmental considerations into urban planning are all ways in which comprehensive energy and environmental policies can strengthen the Gulf's position as a responsible global player and ensure a sustainable legacy for future generations.

Soft power strategies: strengthening global influence

Soft power, or the ability to influence through attraction and persuasion, has become an increasingly important aspect of global politics and international relations. In the context of the Gulf region, strengthening soft power strategies is essential to increase global influence and foster constructive relations with nations around the world.

As Gulf leaders navigate the complexities of a rapidly changing geopolitical landscape, effectively deploying the tools of soft power to build trust, cultivate goodwill and shape positive perceptions is imperative. Let's look at the multifaceted soft power strategies and examine how the Gulf region can strengthen its global influence.

The Gulf states possess a rich cultural heritage, as evidenced by their arts, traditions, and historical legacy. Leveraging this cultural capital can be a powerful soft power resource, enabling the projection of a compelling narrative that resonates internationally. Investing in the promotion of cultural assets such as museums, festivals, and exchange programmes can foster intercultural understanding and appreciation, thereby strengthening the Gulf's global influence. Additionally, educational diplomacy is an essential element of these strategies. By offering scholarships, facilitating academic exchanges, and establishing renowned educational institutions, the Gulf can attract and educate future global leaders, thus consolidating its position as a centre of knowledge and innovation. Collaborative research and development initiatives can also amplify the region's intellectual influence, stimulate progress in various fields, and bolster its soft power. Beyond culture and education, economic interdependence and trade alliances are powerful tools for cultivating soft power. By fostering mutually beneficial economic partnerships, the Gulf can demonstrate its reliability, stability and prosperity, thereby inspiring trust and respect on the international stage. Adopting sustainable practices and launching initiatives in renewable energy and environmental management will further strengthen the region's influence, establishing it as a responsible global player committed to solving urgent global issues. Furthermore, supporting humanitarian efforts and contributing to international development aid strengthens the Gulf's credibility and underscores its commitment to human well-being worldwide. In an era of interconnectedness and interdependence, the judicious use of digital and media diplomacy is essential for shaping perceptions and narratives. Leveraging cutting-edge communication technologies and engaging in constructive dialogue enables the Gulf to amplify the reach of its soft power, counter misperceptions and foster inclusive global conversations. Embracing transparency and openness in information dissemination strengthens the region's credibility and reliability, thereby increasing its soft power influence. Ultimately, the strategic orchestration of these elements of soft power is essential for the Gulf to become a respected global player capable of shaping discourse, building lasting partnerships, and contributing significantly to humanity's collective progress.

Youth engagement: empowering the next generation

When considering the future of the Gulf region, it is becoming increasingly clear that young people will play a central role in its evolution. Youth engagement is not only a matter of social inclusion, but also a strategic imperative for the region's sustainable development and stability. Empowering the next generation requires fostering an environment in which young people are actively involved in decision-making processes, encouraged to pursue education and develop their skills, and offered meaningful opportunities to contribute to society.

Investment in education and vocational training is an essential aspect of this empowerment. This equips them with the knowledge and skills needed to thrive in an ever-changing economic landscape, building a competitive and agile workforce in the process. Furthermore, integrating entrepreneurship and innovation into education programmes can stimulate creativity and leadership, enabling young people to become drivers of future growth and prosperity.

Alongside education, it is crucial to provide young people with opportunities for meaningful civic participation. Involving them in community development projects, volunteering initiatives, and governance processes instils a sense of responsibility, empowering them to take ownership of their actions while cultivating their leadership skills and fostering a culture of collaboration. Additionally, providing platforms for dialogue and representation allows young people to express their views on issues that directly affect their lives, promoting a more responsive and inclusive society.

Empowerment also involves addressing the specific challenges faced by young people, such as accessing affordable housing, healthcare, and employment opportunities. Implementing targeted policies and programmes that address these needs can mitigate the risk of social alienation and disengagement, fostering a sense of belonging and investment in the future of the Gulf.

Moreover, using digital technologies and social media as tools for engagement and expression can amplify young people's voices, providing them with a means to express themselves constructively and actively. Digital literacy and the creation of safe online spaces enable young people to leverage connectivity and information sharing to shape discourse and influence public debate on issues that matter to their generation.

Ultimately, empowering the next generation is a strategic investment in the region's long-term viability, not just a matter of philanthropy. By recognising young people's potential as agents of positive change and providing them with necessary support, resources, and opportunities, Gulf leaders can cultivate a dynamic and resilient society ready to confidently and determinedly navigate the complexities of the future.

Policy evaluation and feedback mechanisms

Policy development is an ongoing process that requires regular evaluation and feedback to ensure its effectiveness and relevance. In the context of the Gulf region, where rapid socio-economic and geopolitical changes are reshaping the landscape, it is imperative that leaders establish robust evaluation frameworks and channels for gathering feedback from various stakeholders. The importance of policy evaluation and feedback mechanisms in fostering adaptive and responsive governance is beyond doubt.

A comprehensive policy evaluation framework must encompass several dimensions, including economic impact, social cohesion, environmental sustainability and national security. Integrating diverse perspectives and expertise enables policymakers to gain a comprehensive understanding of the outcomes and implications of their decisions. Using interdisciplinary research and data-driven analysis can contribute to evidence-based policymaking, thereby strengthening the credibility and effectiveness of strategic choices.

Furthermore, establishing transparent and accessible feedback mechanisms is essential to fostering participatory governance and generating a sense of ownership among the population. This involves creating platforms for open dialogue, public consultation, and stakeholder engagement to capture the nuanced realities and aspirations of different societal groups. Digital technologies and social media can facilitate real-time feedback loops, enabling policymakers to assess public opinion and concerns immediately.

It is also important to integrate performance assessments and impact analyses into the policy implementation process. This enables policymakers to adjust their approach and adapt their strategies in response to evolving challenges and opportunities by regularly monitoring and evaluating key performance indicators. Embracing a culture of continuous improvement enables leaders to adapt to changing socio-political landscapes and demonstrate accountability to their constituents.

Another crucial aspect of effective policy evaluation is considering long-term sustainability and resilience. Policies should be evaluated not only in terms of short-term gains, but also from a forward-looking perspective that anticipates potential future implications and risks. This requires scenario planning, risk assessments, and forward-looking analysis to ensure that policies are robust and adaptable in the face of uncertainty and change.

Furthermore, focusing on foresight and strategic anticipation can mitigate unintended consequences and strengthen the strategic coherence of policy choices overall.

In conclusion, robust policy evaluation and feedback mechanisms are essential for making informed decisions, establishing adaptive governance, and gaining public trust in leaders. Prioritising transparency, inclusivity, and foresight enables Gulf leaders to address complex challenges with agility and vision, ultimately leading their societies towards a sustainable and prosperous future.

12
Conclusion
Uncertain Horizons and the Path Forward

Summary of key themes

The introduction provides an overview of the recent geopolitical changes affecting the Gulf region. Reflecting on the issues discussed in this book, it is evident that the Gulf region is at a pivotal point, grappling with multifaceted challenges that carry significant implications. The interaction of historical, economic, security and environmental factors has shaped the current landscape, highlighting the complexity of the issues at stake. By examining the historical context, we have explored the Gulf's pivotal role in global politics, traced the evolution of its relations with major powers and analysed the shifting dynamics of influence and control. The discussion on hydrocarbon dependence and economic diversification has also emphasised the urgent need for Gulf states to transition to sustainable, diversified economies in the face of uncertainties in the global energy market. Furthermore, the security dilemmas facing Gulf states — who must balance alliances, arms acquisitions, and aspirations for autonomy — have created a web of strategic considerations with significant implications for regional stability. Geopolitical tensions, particularly with Iran and Israel, have added an extra layer of complexity, requiring a delicate balancing act to avoid potential escalation. The impact of the global energy transition, combined with environmental challenges such as climate change, has further exacerbated the situation in the region, prompting the need for proactive measures and innovative solutions. Socio-political dynamics, such as national identity and popular sentiment, have also proven to be key determinants of the future direction of the Gulf region, prompting introspection and adaptation. Exploring the opportunities and obstacles to regional integration has revealed the potential for enhanced cooperation, as well as the barriers hindering progress. In summarising these major themes, it is evident that the Gulf region is confronted with a multitude of interrelated challenges that necessitate comprehensive and forward-looking strategies. This summary will inform further discussions on the way forward, providing valuable insights for policymakers, academics, and other stakeholders involved in the future of the Gulf.

Summary of key challenges

A comprehensive analysis of the Gulf region's multiple geopolitical dimensions is imperative to summarise the key challenges it faces. The interaction between historical legacy, economic dependencies, and security dilemmas has created a multitude of challenges with far-reaching implications. At the heart of these challenges lies the region's dependence on hydrocarbons, which has shaped its socio-political dynamics, economic structures, and international relations. This dependence leaves the region vulnerable to global energy transitions, highlighting the urgent need for diversification. Furthermore, the region's complex network of strategic alliances and rivalries creates a state of permanent uncertainty, necessitating a re-evaluation of diplomatic and security strategies. Geopolitical tensions, particularly with Iran and Israel, exacerbate these complexities further, influencing decision-making processes and prospects for stability. Additionally, environmental challenges such as climate change and sustainability concerns add an extra layer of complexity to the region's future trajectory, emphasising the necessity of proactive and innovative environmental and resource management strategies. Sociopolitical dynamics, such as national identity and public opinion, raise issues relating to social cohesion and government legitimacy. While regional integration offers the prospect of collective progress, it encounters obstacles that require careful consideration and strategic navigation. Thus, summarising the main challenges facing the Gulf requires an understanding of the ways in which issues affecting the economic, political, social and environmental spheres are interrelated. Only through in-depth analysis will it be possible to outline promising paths for the future and set the Gulf region on a course towards greater resilience and sustainability.

Reassessing strategic alliances

Strategic alliances have long played a fundamental role in the geopolitical landscape of the Gulf region. However, as global political and economic dynamics continue to evolve, it is imperative to reassess the role and impact of these alliances. Traditional alliances that have contributed to the region's stability and security may need to be re-evaluated in light of changing priorities and new challenges. It is essential to critically analyse the effectiveness of existing alliances and explore new partnerships to meet the region's evolving needs.

Historically, the Gulf region has relied on strategic alliances with powerful external actors to ensure its security and protect its interests. These alliances have often been reinforced by military cooperation, intelligence sharing, and diplomatic support. However, changing global political dynamics require a comprehensive reassessment of the viability and relevance of these partnerships. In this context, reassessing strategic alliances requires thoroughly analysing the mutual benefits, risks, and long-term implications of each alliance.

Furthermore, the emergence of new regional and international actors has introduced a degree of complexity that necessitates a nuanced approach to alliance-building. The rise of non-traditional security threats, cyber warfare and ideological friction further highlights the need to reconsider strategic alliances. Additionally, the increasing influence of non-state actors and transnational movements is compelling Gulf states to adjust their alliance strategies.

When reassessing strategic alliances, all aspects must be taken into account, including military and security considerations as well as economic, technological and socio-cultural factors. Expanding alliances to encompass areas beyond security and defence cooperation can pave the way for greater economic interdependence, technology transfer and cultural exchange. This expansion could foster greater resilience and adaptability in the face of multifaceted challenges, thereby contributing to the region's long-term stability and prosperity.

Reassessing strategic alliances also enables Gulf states to recalibrate their foreign policies to reflect their evolving national interests and aspirations.

An introspective analysis of the alignment between the objectives of the Gulf states and their allies will enable alliances to be restructured to better serve the collective interests of all stakeholders. Ultimately, reassessing strategic alliances reflects a proactive, forward-looking approach to navigating contemporary geopolitical complexities.

By recognising the fluidity of global power dynamics and strategically repositioning themselves within the context of evolving alliances, Gulf states can adapt to future uncertainties while seizing new opportunities for collaboration and mutual benefit.

Innovations in economic diversification

The Gulf region has long depended on the hydrocarbon industry, but as the global energy transition accelerates, the need for economic diversification is becoming increasingly urgent. Innovations in economic diversification are essential to ensuring a sustainable and resilient future for the region. To achieve this transformation, a proactive approach guided by strategic vision and innovative policies is required. Developing knowledge-based industries such as technology, finance, and advanced manufacturing is a promising way to achieve this. Investing in education, research and development will enable Gulf countries to cultivate a dynamic ecosystem that fosters entrepreneurship, creativity and intellectual capital. Exploiting renewable energy sources also offers an attractive way to stimulate economic diversification while addressing environmental concerns. Expanding solar and wind energy projects and investing in green technologies can reduce dependence on fossil fuels, stimulate job growth and attract sustainable investment. Collaboration between the public and private sectors is essential to stimulate innovation and foster an environment conducive to economic diversification. Strategic partnerships with global technology hubs can facilitate knowledge transfer, skills development, and the adoption of best practices. Additionally, fostering a culture of innovation and entrepreneurship through favourable regulatory frameworks, financing mechanisms, and incubation centres can encourage the development of new industries and start-ups. Encouraging the growth of small and medium-sized enterprises (SMEs) is essential, as they often drive innovation and job creation. Gulf states can foster their growth by providing tailored support, access to finance and simplified regulation, enabling them to contribute significantly to economic diversification. Government initiatives to develop specialised economic zones and industrial clusters can also promote economic diversification, attract foreign investment, and encourage trade. Finally, it is crucial that diversification efforts align with sustainable development goals. A focus on social inclusion, responsible environmental management and ethical business practices will ensure that diversification strategies stimulate economic growth and improve societal well-being while preserving the region's natural heritage. As the Gulf navigates the complexities of economic diversification, adopting innovations across various sectors will pave the way for a dynamic and resilient future characterised by prosperity, sustainability, and inclusive development.

Adapting to energy transitions

As the global energy landscape undergoes rapid and transformative changes, countries in the Gulf region must adapt to these transitions. Historically dependent on hydrocarbon resources for the backbone of their economies, Gulf states must now diversify their energy portfolios and recalibrate their economic strategies. This requires a multifaceted approach combining innovation, policy reform and strategic vision.

A thorough reassessment of the energy mix is one of

the key aspects of this adaptation. Sustained efforts are needed to integrate renewable energy sources into existing infrastructure, thereby promoting a more balanced and sustainable energy ecosystem. At the same time, investment in the research and development of alternative energy technologies is vital for a successful transition. Furthermore, developing partnerships with international entities and leveraging expertise in sustainable energy practices will strengthen the Gulf's position in the evolving global energy landscape.

Another crucial element of this adaptation is reconfiguring economic structures. Transforming hydrocarbon-based economies requires a strategic shift towards knowledge-based, innovative, and entrepreneurial sectors. This requires targeted investment in education, technology, and human capital to propel the region towards a more resilient and diversified economic landscape. It is also essential to foster an environment conducive to innovation and entrepreneurship through regulatory reforms and incentives, ensuring a sustainable economic transformation.

Beyond technological and economic considerations, adapting to energy transitions requires comprehensive policy frameworks that prioritise environmental sustainability. Stricter regulations on emissions, natural resource conservation, and sustainable urban planning are vital for mitigating the environmental impact of energy production and consumption. Adopting circular economy principles and green practices across all sectors would further strengthen the Gulf's commitment to environmental preservation.

In conclusion, the Gulf region requires visionary leadership, strategic foresight and proactive governance to adapt to energy transitions. Embracing this transition will strengthen the region's resilience, boost its global competitiveness, and establish the groundwork for a sustainable and prosperous future.

Projections for regional stability

Projections for regional stability in the Gulf are shaped by a complex interplay of geopolitical, economic, and social factors. As the context of growing uncertainty takes hold, it becomes imperative to thoroughly analyse the various dimensions contributing to the region's future stability.

One of the key determinants of regional stability is the evolving balance of power and influence between Gulf states and their global allies. The reconfiguration of alliances and partnerships in response to changing geopolitical realities will undoubtedly affect this balance. As traditional and emerging powers seek to consolidate their positions, the balance between competition and cooperation will determine the future regional landscape.

Furthermore, the Gulf's security architecture is closely linked to regional stability. Ongoing conflicts and proxy wars have profound implications for the entire Gulf region, affecting security and stability. Understanding the factors driving these conflicts and the prospects for resolution is essential for predicting the evolution of regional stability.

Economic diversification and sustainable development also play a crucial role in achieving this. As countries seek to reduce their dependence on hydrocarbons and diversify their economies, transitioning to knowledge- and innovation-based economies will be critical in addressing socio-economic challenges and promoting stability. Additionally, investing in sustainable development and environmental preservation initiatives will contribute to the region's long-term stability.

Furthermore, social and demographic dynamics within the Gulf states are a key factor to consider when forecasting regional stability. Youth empowerment, social cohesion, cultural diversity, and inclusive governance will significantly impact the resilience and stability of Gulf societies. It is essential to understand the population's aspirations and concerns in order to develop policies and strategies that promote social harmony and stability.

In future, the stability of the Gulf region will also be influenced by external forces, including shifts in global power, technological advances and evolving international engagement norms. Anticipating the impact of these influences on regional stability is essential for implementing proactive measures to address potential destabilising factors.

In conclusion, the outlook for regional stability in the Gulf is inextricably linked to geopolitical, economic, security and societal complexities.

By carefully analysing and anticipating these multifactorial elements, stakeholders can better understand possible pathways to strengthening stability and resilience in the region.

Implications for sustainable development

Ensuring sustainable development in this region is essential to guaranteeing its long-term prosperity and stability. The region's unique geopolitical, economic, and environmental landscape has multiple implications for sustainable development. Preserving natural resources such as water and arable land is vital for ensuring sustainable agricultural practices and food security. Additionally, diversifying the economy to reduce reliance on hydrocarbons is crucial for ensuring sustainable growth and navigating the global energy transition. This requires investment in renewable energy, technological innovation, and the development of human capital to foster a knowledge-based economy.

Effective governance and strategic planning are key to sustainable development. Clear policy frameworks and regulations must be established to promote sustainable resource management, environmental conservation and social equity. Integrating sustainability principles into urban planning, infrastructure development and industrial activities mitigates environmental degradation and promotes economic growth. Furthermore, encouraging sustainable consumption patterns and good waste management practices helps to relieve pressure on natural resources and reduce the ecological footprint.

Sustainable development also has a profound impact on societal well-being and quality of life. Focusing on social development initiatives such as education, healthcare and affordable housing helps enrich human capital and stabilise society. Inclusive socio-economic policies that prioritise employment, gender equality and social well-being are essential for fostering cohesive and resilient communities. Investing in ecotourism and cultural heritage preservation supports sustainable economic growth and enriches the region's cultural identity.

Environmental preservation and tackling climate change are integral to sustainable development. The Gulf region faces unique environmental challenges, including desertification, water scarcity and extreme temperatures, requiring proactive measures to mitigate the impact of climate change. In order to ensure climate resilience, renewable energy solutions must be implemented, water conservation practices improved and sustainable land use promoted. Adopting international best practices and making commitments to reduce carbon emissions and increase environmental sustainability is paramount to ensuring the region's future viability.

In conclusion, sustainable development in the Gulf region has considerable implications for various aspects of governance, the economy, society and the environment. A holistic approach to sustainable development involves addressing complex challenges and seizing opportunities in a coordinated manner. By integrating sustainability principles into policymaking, investment strategies and social welfare, Gulf countries can move towards a more sustainable and resilient future.

Pathways and scenarios

The future of the Gulf region is marked by unprecedented uncertainty and complexity. As we navigate a rapidly changing geopolitical landscape, scenario planning emerges as an essential tool for anticipating and preparing for multiple possible futures. This process involves imagining different, plausible yet divergent narratives in order to capture the full range of potential uncertainties and disruptions. By considering these scenarios, decision-makers can adopt a strategic position and respond effectively to the unpredictable forces that will shape the future of the Gulf region. It is crucial to evaluate the impact of the global energy transition on the region's hydrocarbon-dependent economies and to plan alternative routes towards sustainable development. This requires a proactive commitment to renewable energy, economic diversification, and investment in technology and innovation. At the same time, however, scenario planning must also take into account the region's complex security challenges and power dynamics, as well as the potential implications of shifting alliances, regional conflicts, and external interventions. This necessitates a nuanced understanding of geopolitical fault lines and opportunities for de-escalation and cooperation. Options for the future must also include a thorough analysis of societal and cultural changes, taking into account evolving national identities, demographic transitions, and societal aspirations. Scenarios should also consider the potential impact of technological advances, demographic changes, and civil society dynamics on the region's socio-political fabric. In light of climate change and environmental degradation, scenario planning must also outline strategies and policies aimed at mitigating risks and promoting ecological resilience. As we consider the paths forward, it is imperative to engage in structured debate to anticipate highly probable yet uncertain trajectories that could shape the Gulf in the coming decades. Through rigorous scenario planning, policymakers and stakeholders can develop a comprehensive understanding of the dynamic interplay of factors that will influence the future. This will support them in making informed decisions and developing resilient strategies to address the uncertain horizons ahead.

Lessons for policymakers

As we conclude our in-depth exploration of the Gulf's geopolitical landscape, it is crucial to identify key takeaways for policymakers who are responsible for guiding the region through its future complexities and challenges. The complex interplay of historical legacies, regional rivalries, economic dependencies and global dynamics underscores the need for a nuanced, adaptive approach to policymaking in the region. One of the key lessons to be drawn from our analysis is the critical importance of diversifying national economies to mitigate the risks associated with excessive dependence on hydrocarbon resources. Policymakers would be well advised to respond to the call for sustained efforts to encourage innovation, entrepreneurship, and investment beyond the energy sector. This would lay the foundations for a sustainable and resilient economic future. Furthermore, the evolving nature of global energy transitions requires Gulf leaders to take a proactive stance, demonstrating strategic foresight and investing in renewable energy and clean technologies. This transition offers policymakers the chance to embrace innovation and adopt new energy production and consumption paradigms, positioning their countries at the forefront of the global shift towards sustainable development. Another key lesson is the need to recalibrate existing regional alliances to reflect the changing geopolitical landscape. They must navigate the complex web of alliances and rivalries with caution, recognising that maintaining stability and security requires shrewd diplomacy, dialogue, and multilateral cooperation. Furthermore, in the face of the looming threat of climate change, policymakers must prioritise environmental sustainability and climate resilience, integrating these considerations into their long-term planning and decision-making processes. The lessons learned in this chapter emphasise the necessity of visionary leadership, collaboration, and an unwavering commitment to the well-being and prosperity of the region's inhabitants. Policymakers must internalise these lessons and chart a course that transcends immediate challenges, promoting a vision of the Gulf as a model of progress, stability, and good governance.

Conclusions and outlook

As we conclude this study, it is crucial to consider the implications of our findings for the future of the Gulf region. The interplay of geopolitics, energy dynamics and societal forces highlights the need for a holistic and forward-looking approach to navigating the uncertainties ahead. Looking to the future, it is evident that strategic foresight, adaptive governance and proactive collaboration are crucial for achieving sustainable development and stability.

Beyond the immediate challenges, there is an urgent need to implement innovative policies that anticipate and respond to the repercussions of global energy transitions. Economic diversification, as well as investment in renewable energy and sustainable technologies, will help to mitigate the risks associated with excessive reliance on hydrocarbons. Additionally, fostering partnerships and dialogue between Gulf states, regional actors, and international stakeholders can enhance prospects for harmonious coexistence and mutual prosperity.

To do so, we must learn from past strategies and experiences. The balance of power in the region, the effects of historical conflicts, and the evolving nature of alliances all serve to highlight the complexity of the Gulf's geopolitical landscape. Therefore, it will be crucial to adjust diplomatic commitments, rethink security doctrines and redefine national aspirations in order to assert the role of Gulf countries and address new challenges with resolute pragmatism.

This moment in history demands a collective commitment to sustainable and inclusive progress. Pursuing a path that prioritises environmental stewardship, social cohesion, and economic balance will require courageous leadership and dynamic policymaking. The ability to envisage alternative scenarios, prepare for disruptive change, and leverage innovation for renewal will be crucial in ensuring the Gulf region's future resilience and prosperity.

Finally, our forward-looking reflections should foster optimism and ambition and inspire constructive dialogue about the opportunities available to Gulf countries. By sharing best practices, opening new avenues of cooperation and upholding shared values, the region's diverse communities can redefine resilience and write a new chapter in their history, one marked by triumph over adversity. The next chapters of the region's history are yet to be written, and it is up to leaders, visionaries, and changemakers to collectively shape an era characterised by progress, peace, and prosperity.

About the authors

Bernard Badie and Chedli Mustapha are two French entrepreneurs who have been based in the Gulf for several years. This book is the result of their collaboration and shared experience. It will be of interest to anyone interested in the future of the Gulf Cooperation Council member states, from economic, environmental or geopolitical perspectives.

www.ingramcontent.com/pod-product-compliance
Lightning Source LLC
Chambersburg PA
CBHW031148020426
42333CB00013B/560